PERSO

The Department at Work

The Author

Penny Hackett MA, PhD, FIPM, is Company Training and Development Manager at Clarks International, based in Somerset. Previously Course Director for personnel management courses at Kingston Business School and a member of the Institute of Personnel Management National Education Committee, she is still actively involved in the development of IPM work at the University of the West of England and Bridgwater College.

Educated at St Anne's College Oxford and Kingston Polytechnic, she has experience of personnel and training in organizations spanning the service and manufacturing, public and private sectors. She has been involved in a wide range of consultancy activities and carried out research into how newly qualified personnel practitioners get jobs.

She has written a number of books and articles, including *Success in Management: Personnel* (John Murray), *Interview Skills Training: Practice Packs for Trainers* (IPM) and *Choosing the Players*, part of the IPM series on Managing People in the Small and Growing Business.

Audio Cassette

The issues discussed in this book are developed further in an audio cassette, also entitled **Personnel: The department at work.** This includes interviews with Penny Hackett and the former Director General of the IPM as well as five dramatized sections exploring the basic principles and techniques of:

- selection interviews
- appraisals
- disciplinary procedures
- putting the case for training
- collective bargaining.

Supplementing the information contained in this book, it provides realistic and absorbing examples of all the key personnel functions and offers ample material for further discussion and debate. It is equally useful for careers officers, in-company trainers, business studies students – and anyone considering a career in personnel.

PERSONNEL
The Department at Work

Penny Hackett

Cartoons and cover by
rich

Institute of Personnel Management

First published in 1991
Reprinted 1994

Phototypeset by Paragon Photoset, Aylesbury
and printed in Great Britain by
Biddles Ltd of Guildford

British Library Cataloguing in Publication Data

Hackett, Penny
  Personnel.
  1. Personnel. Management
  I. Title   II. Institute of Personnel Management
  658.3

ISBN 0-85292-458-5

ipm

INSTITUTE OF PERSONNEL MANAGEMENT
IPM House, Camp Road, Wimbledon, London SW19 4UX
Tel: 081-946-9100   Fax: 081-947-2570
Registered office as above. Registered Charity No. 215797
A company limited by guarantee. Registered in England No. 198002

Contents

Foreword

Personnel management can provide a very satisfying and rewarding career. It is one which can be followed in many different types of organization and which includes many different facets. It is also a demanding career, which requires much more than good intentions and a wish to 'work with people'.

The Work of the Personnel Department is intended to give an insight into what is involved. It is designed for:

- those who are choosing a career for the first time and need to 'get the feel' of what life in personnel is like;
- those who are at a turning point in their careers and feel that personnel may offer a way forward;
- those whose aim is to join an established personnel department within a medium-sized or large organization;
- those who wish to build up the personnel elements within a more general administrative role in a small organization.

It is not an academic text. Nor is it a detailed 'how to do it' guide. My aim throughout has been to provide a flavour of the sort of activities which make up the work of the personnel department – and to paint a realistic picture of it. Each of the main chapters includes a 'Who can Help?' section, to point you in the direction of in-depth advice and reading on particular topics. There is also a guide to more general texts on page 175.

If, after reading it, you decide that a career in personnel is not really for you after all, the book will have served a useful purpose. I hope you will enjoy whatever alternative career you decide to pursue. If, on the other hand, you feel you *would* like to work in personnel, I hope the advice in Chapter Ten will help to get you started.

Penny Hackett

Chapter One

What *is* Personnel Management?

Introduction

If you are thinking of starting work in a personnel department, the first thing you will want to know is 'what's it all about?'. What is the department there for? What does it actually *do*? If the 'department' is bigger than a one-man (or woman) band – who does what?

As you would expect, the answers to such questions are likely to vary between organizations – depending not only on obvious things like their size, ownership and purpose, but also on more subtle differences in culture and values. In some small organizations, personnel work may be combined with other things – general administration or involvement in the work of a company secretary for instance. In very big organizations, some of the things which we treat here as part of the work of *the* personnel department may in fact be separated out under different company directors.

If we stop too often to take account of these variations, this first chapter particularly will be very full of 'if's' and 'but's' – which would not make for easy reading. So instead, we will steer a middle course, taking as our mental model a reasonably progressive, medium-sized personnel department, in a reasonably progressive, medium-sized company.

What's it all About?

Personnel Management is about managing people at work. It is about the relationship between each individual employee and his or her employer. It is also about the collective relationship between *all* the employees in a particular organization and their employer.

Managing people at work is something which *all* managers

do. Everyone who is responsible for getting work done through other people needs to decide:

- how many people are needed
- how best to divide the work between them
- where to find people who are ready, willing and able to do the work
- how to persuade them to join the organization, and how to keep them working effectively for it
- what to do to help people to keep pace with the changing needs of the organization
- how to deal with the problems which arise when the number or the skills of the people working for the organization are out of line with its future requirements.

In all but the smallest organizations, some of these decisions are arrived at with the help of a personnel department.

Later in this chapter we will examine how these 'personnel' aspects of management can be divided between line managers (who have direct responsibility for a particular part of the business and direct authority over the people who work for them), and personnel specialists. As we shall see, both must pool their efforts to enable all those who work for the organization to make their own best contribution to its success.

What is the Department there *For*?

To answer this question we need to think

- why it is necessary to pay attention to people at work in the first place;
- why line managers may need help in doing this;
- why it may be better if that help is provided by *specialists*, as well as by their line bosses.

We will explore each in turn.

1. Your organization needs to pay attention to people at work because a well-trained, highly motivated, well-coordinated

team is much more effective than an ill-informed, apathetic, misdirected bunch of individuals. But well-trained, highly motivated, well-coordinated teams *are* made up of individuals, each with a mind of his or her own. Within the constraints of their skills, abilities and aspirations, each is free to choose what job to do, where to do it, and, up to a point, how well to do it.

Successful organizations recognize this and give constant attention to finding the best ways of getting, developing and keeping the people they need, in the right numbers and in the right places. Unsuccessful organizations suffer alternately from skill shortages and overmanning – and, as a result, can never take full advantage of business opportunities.

Careful attention to people at work can prove valuable in other ways too. For most organizations, the cost of wages, benefits, training and so forth is one of the most expensive items they must meet. Soundly researched and well-structured 'people' policies can mean that this expenditure becomes an investment paying handsome dividends. Poor handling will result in money down the drain as skilled employees leave and time is lost through disputes and grievances.

In addition, most organizations set great store by their public image, believing (rightly) that this can have a major impact on their ability to do business. The organization whose 'people' policies are in line with the best professional standards will tend to have a more favourable image. Certainly, the one which consistently attracts adverse media comment, perhaps as a result of flouting health and safety or equal opportunities law, will have low public credibility.

2. The line managers in your organization may need help in devising and following good 'people' policies because, in the hurly-burly of day to day business activity, problems tend to be immediate and many managers feel they are under pressure to find instant solutions. In such an environment, the longer term consequences of sacking Mary or giving Jake a pay rise may not be uppermost in their boss' mind. Busy line managers, preoccupied with the demands of production or sales, may need the support and advice of someone not directly involved.

What is needed in such situations is *consistency*.

Consistency is vital in dealing with people. People don't mind working hard – as long as they can see that everyone else is working hard too.

People don't mind working hard – as long as they can see that everyone else is working hard too . . .

People don't mind being asked to stick to the rules – as long as they can see that the rules – and the consequences of breaking them – are the same for everyone.

Consistency doesn't necessarily mean equality. People don't mind being paid less than the managing director – as long as they can see that there is a logical reason for the difference. If it *fairly* reflects differences in the demands made on the job holder, and/or in the contribution he or she makes, it will not be resented.

Unless somewhere in the organization someone is striving to establish such consistency of treatment, people problems may become a very real constraint on success.

3. The main reason why that 'someone' should be a personnel specialist, rather than another member of line management, is that it takes some time to acquire the knowledge and skills needed to do the job properly. ('Doing the job properly' implies that some sort of consistent framework of policies and procedures must be devised, to help guide line managers.

If full benefit is to be obtained, the framework must not only fit with the internal needs of the organization – it must be legal and cost effective as well.)

The key areas of knowledge include:

- human behaviour (individual and in groups)
- employment law
- government manpower policies
- specialist processes and techniques – from human resource planning to pay and benefits and from recruitment and selection to the design and evaluation of training.

Among the key skills are:

- interpersonal skills – for negotiating, interviewing and counselling
- analytical and evaluative skills – for assessing job candidates and interpreting behaviour and information
- written and spoken communication skills – for training and development and to 'make the case' for effective people policies
- creative skills – for designing imaginative approaches to communication and training.

Many other managers may have some of this knowledge and skill. But it would be a tall order to expect someone who must also specialize in another function, be it finance, marketing, production or operations, to acquire *all* of them in real breadth and depth.

What Does the Personnel Department *Do*?

In the past, 'personnel management' was often seen as just a grander sounding name for 'welfare'. The personnel specialist was regarded as a do-gooder, who helped to square the corporate conscience when there were difficult decisions to be made.

To help shake off this image, and to signal a much more positive role, many personnel departments are now being renamed Human Resource Departments. We will explore the implications of this more fully later. Here, it is important for us to note that the emphasis in personnel management is changing and that the activities in which personnel departments are involved are increasingly designed to reflect the importance of people as an investment and a resource, rather than as an expensive overhead cost.

There are seven key types of activity you can expect to find in a personnel department. As we shall see, not everyone will be involved in all of them – and the precise nature of the work you will be expected to do when you join a personnel department will depend on the level to which you are appointed. We will consider each broad area of activity in turn, in the order in which a newly introduced personnel department might need to tackle them, then we will examine the different levels at which each may be carried out.

1. Corporate Planning

Unless the senior management of your organization know what they want the business to look like in three to five years' time, the chances are it will drift, sooner rather than later, into oblivion.

Their plans may be systematically enshrined in a formal document, with carefully thought out strategies for achieving clearly defined objectives – for market share, turnover, profit, number of outlets, number of employees, and the like. Or, their plans may be scribbled on the back of a cigarette packet. Either way, the 'people' implications of the plans are vital.

If an organization wishes to move ahead, it must first work out what the options are – in terms of market opportunities. When it comes to choosing between alternative options, it would be a foolhardy chief executive who would disregard the skills and interests of the existing workforce. True, new people can be recruited, and existing staff can be retrained or fired. But these may be very expensive courses of action.

At the very least, these costs should be calculated and taken into account before deciding to proceed. The personnel specialist can contribute to the corporate planning process by highlighting the people implications of alternative business options.

2. Organization

In all but the very smallest enterprises, you will find some form of subdivision of activities. As soon as the operation becomes too big for one person to manage, separate *divisions* or *departments* are likely to be created, to focus on different parts of the overall business activity.

Among the most common forms of this is departmentation by *function* – that is, a marketing division, a manufacturing division, a finance division, a personnel division, and so forth. Alternatively, you may find a northern division, a southern division, an eastern and a western division – that is *geographical* departmentation – or, in a local authority for example, a housing department, an education department, a social services department – that is departmentation by *product*.

Within each of these major groupings you are likely to find many smaller departments – each with a manager and perhaps some supervisors.

During the last hundred years, much time and thought has been devoted to working out how best to tackle this problem of subdivision. How many people should a manager manage? How many *levels* of management should there be? How *should* the organization be divided up – by function, by geography, by product – or what?

Because no-one has yet found the 'right' answers to these questions, in many organizations a lot of time and energy is spent on regular 'restructuring'. This can be a confusing and sometimes painful process for those caught up in it, and calls for careful planning and effective communication.

While the personnel department may not always *initiate* such changes, it is well placed to assess their implications and to work out how to help other members of the organization to come to terms with change.

3. Human Resource Planning

There are few things more frustrating than finding that market opportunities cannot be seized because there simply aren't enough skilled people available to grasp them. But overmanning can be every bit as damaging as a shortage of skills. Employing two people where one, or one plus a machine, could do the job as effectively and more cheaply, just doesn't make sound business sense.

In any large and complex organization, getting the right people in the right place at the right time doing the right things takes a lot of careful planning. This planning process starts with a careful assessment of future human resource needs and current availability. Only when this has been done can sensible decisions be made about when and how much you need to recruit, train, retrain, transfer, or reduce the numbers employed.

The formulation of a human resource plan requires input from many different parts of the organization. Line managers must be helped to make accurate assessments of future needs. Accurate personnel department records can form the basis of the statistical calculations needed to formulate future requirements and to monitor progress towards meeting them. Personnel specialists will also be closely involved in putting the plan into operation – through recruitment, training and dismissal procedures.

4. Training and Development

Unlike many other resources, people can become more

valuable over time. As their skills and knowledge increase, they can work more quickly and achieve higher standards.

Few people like to feel that they are stagnating, plodding through the same routine day after day. But few people really enjoy being completely out of their depth, struggling to cope with tasks they haven't the first idea how to tackle.

Constant attention to the training and development of the workforce enables an organization to keep pace with the changing world – while making the most of the investment it has already made in its human resources.

For every line manager, the development of a competent and committed team should be a top priority. On-job training and coaching play a key part in many organizations' training strategies. Many organizations also make sure that line managers take a leading role in designing and running off-job training courses.

Personnel specialists can help to analyse who needs training, and in what. They can design training materials to be used by line managers. They may also pass on specialist skills like interviewing, presentation and training skills. They can research the ever-growing collection of external courses and specialist training services available through colleges and consultancy firms. They can provide the framework for the evaluation of training. In short, they can help to make training and development a way of life for those whose continually developing skills are at the core of their employer's business.

5. Rewards

The development of a clear and coherent pay and benefits policy lets employees know what they can expect of their employer. Confusion over rewards and feelings of injustice can undo all the hard work that may have gone into attracting and developing an effective team.

Many factors will influence the policy. Personnel's role will be to research the options and to work with senior managers to develop a policy which accurately reflects the values of the organization.

Once the policy is clear, pay and benefits structures can be agreed and personnel can take over the day to day administration of both. In some organizations this means that personnel get involved in the administration of company car schemes, health insurance, staff uniforms and other benefits. In others, such activities are handled elsewhere.

6. Employee Relations

Maintaining good relations with employees reduces the time wasted in disputes and strikes. It can also contribute more positively by creating the kind of climate where people want to give their best.

Firm but fair disciplinary and grievance procedures for tackling individual problems will help to create such a climate. So too will clear and coherent policies on issues such as health and safety and equal opportunities. Where there is a significant level of trade union membership among employees, it will also be necessary to set up machinery for negotiating with union representatives to tackle collective disputes and to determine pay and other employment conditions.

One of the keys to maintaining harmonious working relationships is consistency. And, as we have seen, consistency is something which personnel specialists are well placed to provide. They can ensure that precedents set in one part of the organization are communicated to and followed in other parts.

The line manager will be responsible for the quality of day to day relationships in his or her part of the business. But the overall climate of employee relations will owe much to the skill of those directly involved in trade union negotiations. In many industrial organizations, this forms a major part of the work of the personnel department.

7. Employee Services

Some employers believe that their obligations to their employees start and finish with the terms of their contract of employment. Others take the view that a more broadly based concern for the *quality* of working life is important.

Those in the latter category are likely to provide a wide range of additional services for their employees. These may include counselling to help deal with stress or to resolve personal or domestic problems, and/or facilities such as creches, canteens, sports and social clubs, health screening, staff loans and other 'welfare' arrangements.

The welfare aspect of personnel is often the one which shapes people's expectations of the personnel department. Indeed, some people feel drawn to the profession because they see it as a chance to help others. Many line managers feel more comfortable passing personal or domestic problems over to someone who is not directly involved with the employee on a day to day basis – so tend to load 'welfare' problems onto the personnel department.

The provision of employee services is an important part of progressive employment policies. For many people working in personnel though, the workload associated with the other six areas of activity we have listed tends to mean that 'welfare' is only a small part of their job.

Who Does What?

From our discussion so far, it should be clear that all the work of the personnel department is done *with* line managers. The exact allocation of responsibilities between the two will of course vary from one organization to another and from one area of activity to another.

In some instances, the role of personnel is simply to provide a *service* to line managers, by undertaking routine work which would be too time consuming for line managers to do themselves. The drafting of advertisements and the preliminary sifting of application forms during recruitment are examples.

Quite often, the personnel specialist is in a position to provide advice to line managers – about comparative pay levels, about what should go into the health and safety policy, about whether or not a particular dismissal is likely to result in losing a case at an industrial tribunal. This *advisory* role is perhaps the most usual for the personnel specialist. In it, they have no direct authority over staff in other departments and the final decision about what to do is left to the line manager.

There are, however, occasions where personnel has authority to be more directive and adopts what is sometimes referred to as an *audit* role. Just as a financial auditor checks up to make sure there are no breaches of the procedures for handling money, so from time to time personnel specialists may check on the extent to which the company's procedures for handling people are being adhered to. Those who are found to be paying their staff more than they should, or who are not complying with the equal opportunities policy may be told to mend their ways.

In some instances, the personnel department wields even greater power, and *can* make decisions which directly affect a line manager's staff. Such an *executive* role is most commonly found in the later stages of disciplinary and grievance procedures, where the head of personnel may be the one who makes the final decision about what is to be done.

If you are working within a personnel department, it is important that you understand whether you can make executive decisions or should simply give advice or provide a service. You may find that in some parts of your job you are expected to fulfil one role, while other tasks may require something different.

In some organizations, the debate over which are executive functions and which are advisory functions is superfluous. Where personnel is seen as part of the total management team, the input of the personnel specialist will always be sought by other managers and decisions will be reached jointly. The role of *co-equal professional* enables the personnel specialist to make the maximum contribution to the success of the organization – which is after all his or her overriding purpose.

In such a role, it is possible for personnel to do much more than simply respond to problems identified by others. The co-equal professional can identify what positive steps are needed to help the organization and its people to develop to their full potential. He or she can take the initiative, sounding out new ideas and approaches with colleagues in other parts of the business. Such a *proactive* role is one which many personnel specialists now seek. The extent to which they succeed will depend in no small measure on whether they have the knowledge, skills and general credibility to make their line management colleagues sit up and take notice of them.

So far, we have implied that the only choice of who does

what is between the personnel specialist and the line manager. In fact, in all but the smallest personnel departments there are also decisions to be taken about how the work will be split within the department. This can be done in a number of ways.

Vertical division

There are four main levels at which each of the activities we have discussed can be carried out. Because of the progressively greater knowledge and skill required for dealing with each of the four levels, it is quite common to find a hierarchy of four different levels of personnel specialist.

Personnel Director – – – – – – – – policy
Personnel Manager – – – – – – – – planning
Personnel Officer(s) – – – – – – – operating
Clerical Staff – – – – – – – – – – – clerical

We will look briefly at each level.

Policy. A policy is a framework within which specific decisions can be made. It provides a general guideline and a set of broad principles which can be applied to a number of different situations.

Example: If it is your company's policy to provide equality of opportunity for all present and potential employees, regardless of race, sex, marital status or ethnic origin, you can use this as a principle to guide you whenever you have to make a decision about people. You can ask yourself the question 'if I turn this woman down because she has young children, will I be acting in accordance with company policy?' You will not need a detailed set of rules governing every possible situation in order to work out the answer.

The head of personnel works with top management (usually the board of directors) to develop policy. The policies which they formulate must be closely in tune with the values of the organization. They must also be designed to help achieve its specific objectives – while remaining on the right side of the law and/or at the forefront of good personnel practice. Other members of the organization will find it helpful if policies are written down clearly. Where this is not done there is likely to be confusion at the next level down.

Planning. However clearly stated your company policy is, it may still be helpful to provide more detailed guidance on exactly *how* you should go about making particular decisions.

Example: You will find it easier to put your equal opportunities policy into practice if there is a recruitment procedure which requires each candidate's knowledge and skills to be weighed up against the knowledge and skills needed in the job. If there are procedures for advertising career opportunities to all who may be interested and for making sure that decisions about pay are approached systematically without regard to the sex of the job holder, you will be at least part of the way towards putting your equal opportunities policy into practice.

Designing such procedures is usually the job of a personnel manager, working with middle management elsewhere in the business. Before they begin to plan how the policy will be put into operation, those involved must have a clear view of the objectives they are trying to reach and of the policy which their procedures must serve.

Operating. Once a policy and the relevant procedures have been clearly laid down and people have been trained in their use, it is possible for routine decisions to be made without constant reference to senior management.

Example: If your organization's pay policy is progressively to reward those employees who demonstrate their loyalty and commitment through long service, a simple set of rules can be designed to reflect this. Then, instead of top management time being taken up in deciding who should get a pay rise, someone who knows how the system operates can identify those who are due for an annual increment.

The day to day operation of such procedures is usually the province of the personnel officer, working with managers at all levels in the organization to make sure that procedures are being followed correctly. Only cases which the procedure doesn't seem to fit will need to be referred to the personnel manager.

Clerical. However well policies and procedures have been

devised, and however carefully staff have been trained in their use, no-one will know whether or not they are working unless they are closely monitored. To monitor their effectiveness, accurate information must be kept.

Examples: If your organization has an equal opportunities policy, you will need to record the number of men and women, married and single, black and white – and watch how this changes over time. If your organization has a policy of progressively rewarding those with longer service, you will need to keep accurate records of when people join and how much they are paid. If your organization's personnel policies are designed to reduce the number of people who leave (labour turnover), you will need to record all movements of staff, into and out of the organization.

For all these (and many more) purposes, the storage and retrieval of accurate and up-to-date information about all employees is vital. The clerical staff of the personnel department share this responsibility. The information which they keep provides the basis for management decision-making.

While it is necessary for work to be done at all four of the levels we have discussed, in some organizations you will find a shallower hierarchy. One person may contribute to both policy formulation and setting up procedures, while another is responsible for implementing the procedure and for the clerical aspects. It is even possible to find examples (usually in very small organizations) of one person working at all four levels. In larger organizations, it may be necessary to split work horizontally as well as vertically.

Horizontal division

This can be done in two main ways.

By area of specialist activity. As we have seen, there are seven main areas of personnel activity. It is possible for each of these to be treated as a specialism in its own right and for the work of the personnel department to be divided up accordingly.

The advantage of this is the increased depth of knowledge and skill which people can gain when they specialize in only a small area.

The disadvantage is that many aspects of personnel work are interrelated. Close coordination is therefore needed to avoid duplication of effort or the development of conflicting approaches by different specialists. Figure 1 shows what this might look like.

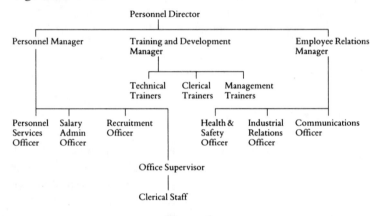

Figure 1

By business/staff function. In order to avoid the problems associated with specialization by area of activity, some organizations divide up the work of the personnel department in a way which mirrors the structure of the organization as a whole.

So one set of specialists may deal with management, another with production workers, a third with clerical employees. Alternatively one set may focus on manufacturing, another on sales and marketing, and another on finance and central services. Figure 2 shows how this might look.

These options reduce the chance of conflict between specialist activities. So it should be possible to ensure that pay policies are compatible with training and development policies and managers aren't asked to undertake performance appraisal interviews while they are in the middle of graduate recruitment.

Careful coordination is still needed though – or you will find that clerical staff are getting longer holiday entitlements than their managers, or those in manufacturing are being sacked for offences which in sales would pass off with only a warning.

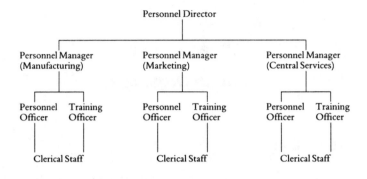

Figure 2

As you would expect, there is no perfect way of splitting up the work of the personnel department. In deciding how best to approach the problem, the size of the organization and the variety of its activities must both be taken into account.

Personnel departments should never be allowed to become so big that they become bureaucratic, pushing around pieces of paper to serve the needs of the personnel department rather than the needs of the organization. Nor should they be split into so many specialisms that the line manager who needs help requires a 'Who's Who' to work out who to talk to.

In common with the rest of the organization, the structure must be kept constantly under review. If the needs of the organization change, the structure of the personnel department can be changed to reflect them.

In later chapters we will look in more detail at what is involved in each of the main specialist areas. But if you are moving into a newly-established personnel role, your first task may be to get the personnel department set up and functioning.

Chapter Two
Getting Organized

Introduction

This chapter is not only for those who will be working in personnel in an organization where the department itself is new. If you do work, or are likely to work in an established personnel department, it will help you to understand why things are organized as they are, and why you have to spend so much time collecting, storing and retrieving information about people.

Setting up a Personnel Department

If you *are* asked to set up a personnel department, it is worth negotiating your role carefully at the outset. If you are working on the assumption that you are in a policy-making, co-equal professional role while everyone else believes you are there as a service providing administrative support, you will be doomed to frustration. If, on the other hand, you believe that you are primarily an administrative service when senior management are looking for a proactive input to the development of personnel policy, your days in personnel could be numbered.

Similarly, if you are alone in perceiving your scope as extending to all the seven areas of activity outlined in Chapter One, you will constantly find yourself accused of meddling in matters that don't concern you. But if you restrict yourself to, say, employee services, when everyone else is expecting you to make a much broader contribution, your boss may want to know the reason why.

During these initial negotiations, you and your chief executive (or other immediate boss) will need to achieve a balance. Perhaps in an ideal world, a chief executive who had identified a need for a personnel department would think carefully about its role, and define precisely what the organization required. He or she would then allow you to suggest what resources – in terms of equipment and/or expertise – were necessary to fulfil this requirement, and make them available to you.

In practice, of course, things rarely happen like that. You may find yourself short of the expertise or resources to make as full a contribution to the organization as you would like. It is far better to confront this early on, and renegotiate the resources – or the role – accordingly, rather than waiting for others to ask why you are falling short.

The role which you agree initially will not necessarily be permanent. A department which starts life providing an administrative service may develop to fulfil other roles, as its contribution is established and the organization, and the staff of the personnel department, develop. Conversely, the department with co-equal professional status may find its role diminishing over time, either because top management have become dissatisfied with the quality of the input provided by personnel, or because other functions begin to see this input as a constraint on their freedom to manage. Then again, the ebbs and flows of organizational politics may mean that areas previously seen as the domain of personnel are taken over by other functions for their own ends.

Your role, and the range and level of activities in which you are expected to become involved, will determine the resources you will need. If you can, negotiate some time to assess exactly what you require and an opportunity to review this after, say, six months.

Try to strike a balance when negotiating resources. You will not gain credibility by empire building. But if you stretch yourself and your people too tightly, something will snap. Whereas some organizations operate quite satisfactorily on a ratio of one personnel specialist to one thousand employees, others work on a ratio closer to one to one hundred. Much depends on the nature of your role – and on the stability of the climate in which you are working. In industries with high labour turnover or poor industrial relations, relatively more resources may be needed to get the situation under control.

Start by listing all the activities in which you expect

your department to get involved. Break each down into its component parts and work out (approximately)

● how long each part takes
● how often it will be repeated.

If, for instance, your department will be involved in recruitment and selection of new employees, you could work out

approximate number of vacancies per year	×	approximate number of interviews per vacancy	×	approximate length of time to interview each candidate

You will then need to add on the time per vacancy spent at other stages in the recruitment and selection process (see Chapter Four), distinguishing, if you can, between tasks which are mainly planning, and those which are operational or clerical (see Chapter One).

If you repeat this process for each of your areas of involvement, you will begin to get at least a broad picture of the time – and therefore the number of people – you will need.

Some areas of activity are much simpler to assess in these terms than others – hence the advice to negotiate a review period. Once your department is in being, it is a lot easier to monitor just how much time is being spent on particular activities – and to modify your estimates accordingly.

Remember, too, that your resources can comprise equipment as well as people. The more automated you are able to make your procedures, the fewer people will be needed. For example, if every contract of employment has to be typed afresh, you will need much more clerical time than if the key paragraphs are stored in a word processor and edited as required. Compare the cost of obtaining the use of computer hardware (equipment) and of acquiring the appropriate software (programs) against the salary and employment costs of extra clerical help, before you make up your mind.

Only if you get the right balance between people and equipment will you be able to provide an efficient service. And providing an efficient service will usually mean being able to provide information and well-founded advice to management – often at very short notice.

Personnel Information

Whatever the role of your department, its credibility will be higher and its task immeasurably easier, if it can

- supply accurate information about employees, quickly and easily
- analyse that information in a way which provides a sound guide to management decision-making.

The sort of questions which line management will expect the personnel department to be able to answer are likely to fall into four broad categories.

1. Questions about individual employees. Where does Henry Joseph live? Which department is Mary Talbot in? What does Arthur Watson do? How old is Rachel Sherman? What do we pay Michael White? When was his last pay review – and when is his next? How many day's absence has Tracy Newman had this year – is there a pattern? Why did Jonathan Hargreaves leave? Can Sheila Graves speak German? Has Tom Nichols attended an interview skills course?

The personnel department is the natural place to go for answers to such questions. To answer them, and others like them, a personal record must be kept for each employee.

2. Questions about groups of employees. How many clerical staff do we employ? How many of them are women? How many of them are paid more than £10,000 per year? How many of them can speak a foreign language? How many of them have been with us for more than one year? How many of them are due to retire by the end of next year? How many days absence do they have, on average, per year? What percentage of them leave us each year? What is their average length of stay before they leave? What are the most frequently occurring reasons for leaving? How much will it cost to give them all a seven per cent pay rise?

These are just some of the questions that may be asked when the effects of specific policies are being reviewed or decisions are to be made about how to make the best use of resources or improve particular aspects of personnel practice. To answer them, it will be necessary to bring together the relevant group of personal records and carry out calculations to produce the required statistics.

3. Questions about policies, procedures and contractual entitlements. What are the rules on compassionate leave? Grace Love has come back from holiday three days late, without a certificate. What can I do? Robert Flight has just sworn at the foreman. Can I sack him? I want to cut my headcount by 20. Do I need to tell the union? I want my staff to do their own cleaning in future. Is there any reason why I shouldn't go ahead and tell them? What is the upper limit on the secretarial pay scale? Angela is worth more than that. How do I pay her?

Again the possible questions are many and varied. To answer them, written statements of terms and conditions for each employee category, a policy and procedures manual, plus copies of agreements reached with trade unions and copies of the pay scales for each category, are needed.

4. Questions about particular areas of activity. How many replies

'I want my staff to do the cleaning in future. Is there any reason why I shouldn't go ahead and tell them?'

did we get last time we advertised in the Argos? How many of the last lot of applicants lived within five miles of here? How many 'no-shows' did we have on the last selection day? How many of the applicants were aged over 30? How long, on average, does it take us to fill a clerical vacancy? How much does it cost? How many training course places have been left unfilled this year? How many delegate training days have we had in the last six months? How much, on average, do we spend training each employee each year? How many substances hazardous to health are in use on our premises? What alternative substances are available? How many days did we lose through strikes last year? How many employee grievances were settled at the first stage of the grievance procedure?

In each of the areas of personnel activity, information about 'what happened last time?' or 'where do we stand on so and so?' is likely to be needed. Although sometimes the answers may be found by reference to information in one of the other three categories, often separate records must be kept to monitor each area.

Anticipating the sort of questions which may be asked, will involve:

- talking to line management – to establish what they feel they *must* know – under each of the four headings we have discussed. If resources permit, you can also invite them to identify what they would *like* to know
- talking to other members of the personnel team
- taking account of the fact that questions may come from outside the organization, as well as inside. The Department of Employment, the Health and Safety Inspectorate, the Equal Opportunities Commission, the Commission for Racial Equality and the Department of Social Security are just some of the bodies who may require information – under any of the categories we have considered.

Collecting the necessary information will involve:

Creating the right 'source' documents. These are likely to include application forms, joiners forms, contracts of employment, a 'changes' form on which variations in pay, hours of work, and other conditions of employment can be notified, absence, accident reporting and self-certification forms, and a leavers form.

Some of these documents, the application form for example, will be completed by individual employees. Others, especially those involving payment and conditions, must be originated by the appropriate line manager and authorized by personnel before being actioned by the payroll department and entered into the employee's personal record. As we shall see in the next section, a computerized personnel information system may reduce the need for paper forms by allowing line managers to update information directly into the system – with appropriate checks and balances.

Updating information. It is simple enough to set up a system for recording changes initiated by the organization. Line managers can be asked to complete a change form or to update a computer record. Keeping up to date with employees' marriages, divorces and acquisition of educational qualifications is not always so easy. It may be necessary to send out a questionnaire or computer printout from time to time, so that people can check the accuracy of the data held, and advise of any changes.

Complying with legislation. 'Data subjects', the people about whom information is stored on a computer, have certain rights under the Data Protection Act 1984. These include the right to inspect the data held, and the right to expect that the information will be used only for authorized purposes. If you intend keeping information in a computerized personnel system, you will need to register with the Data Protection Registrar.

Ensuring confidentiality. Everyone who works in personnel must recognize the importance of this. Information – about individuals or groups of employees – should only ever be released on a 'need to know' basis. It must *never* provide fodder for canteen gossip. Files and computer records must be safeguarded, to prevent any unauthorized access.

Setting up an Information System

Both new and established personnel departments must regularly review the best way of storing the information kept. While some smaller companies still operate 'paper' systems, most larger ones now hold at least part of their personnel information on computer. This means that those who work in the personnel department must not only be able to find their way around the inside of a filing cabinet, they must also be able to use a computer keyboard to input and retrieve information.

Some of the issues which may be involved in setting up a system include:

Choosing the hardware. Will it be appropriate to opt for a 'stand alone' micro computer system exclusive to the personnel department – or should you negotiate for a share of the organization's mainframe?

Deciding the scope of the system. Is it appropriate to take the opportunity to develop one common database (set of computerized information) for use by all the departments who need information about people? Your payroll department, and the pensions department if there is one, may be inputting names, addresses, departments, rates of pay and a host of other data identical to yours. If you have the resources, it makes sense from an organizational viewpoint to link information from all three departments together.

Choosing the software. Will the system be used purely as a means of storing and retrieving data – i.e. a straight alternative to a box of personal record cards? Or will it be used as a means of carrying out complex calculations, modelling alternative courses of action, and automatically generating paper contracts of employment, reports and correspondence?

The most sophisticated systems can do all three. They will manipulate data in accordance with pre-defined formulae which you can set up. So in goes your labour turnover formula with an instruction about which group of employees you are interested in. Out come your labour turnover statistics – perhaps even presented as graphs and bar charts if you have the appropriate software.

If you would like to study the effects of paying everyone adult rates at age 16, you can set up an appropriate instruction and ask the system to tell you the answer. If you like what you see, you can go ahead and implement the change. If you don't, you can try other possibilities or retain the status quo.

If you want to reduce the risk of error and speed up the production of offer letters, invitations to interview, or any other relatively standard correspondence, the technology is available to enable you to 'download' personal data into a word processing system – and produce the required documentation automatically.

Clearly these are all major decisions, involving significant capital investment for your organization. The options must be explored in detail before a decision is made.

Who can Help?

If you are setting up a new department, or overhauling an old one, your investment in the right information system is likely to be one of the most crucial decisions you will have to make. The wrong choice, of hardware or software, is expensive in terms of staff frustration and wasted time – as well as the obvious and considerable cash costs. So do seek specialist advice.

Your best sources are:

Books

For practical advice on how to assess your organization's needs and a directory of the hardware and software packages available, start with

Computerizing Personnel Systems: A basic guide, Alistair Evans, IPM, 1986.

and

Developing a Computerized Personnel System, David Burns Windsor, IPM, 1985.

For illustrated examples of personnel forms and records, consult

Personnel Administration Made Simple: Forms, cards and computers, John Bramham and David Cox, IPM, 1984.

To make sure you stay on the right side of the law, refer to

The Data Protection Act: A guide for personnel managers, Alastair Evans, IPM, 1984.

Courses and Conferences

The Institute of Personnel Management and the Institute of Manpower Studies organize an annual conference on computers in personnel. Details can be obtained from either institute.

Other

Computer manufacturers and software houses will be happy to tell you about their own products and to advise you on their use. Beware the high pressure sales pitch!

Other employers may be prepared to give you the benefit of their experience. If you are considering installing a particular system, always ask the supplier to give the names of other users. Talk to them and if possible visit them to see the system in action. The picture they paint will often be somewhat different from the impression the supplier has tried to create.

Chapter Three

Planning Human Resources

Introduction

Getting the right people, in the right place, at the right time, doing the right things is central to the work of the personnel department. But this does not just happen. It takes careful planning and organizing.

For the newcomer to personnel work, the 'number crunching' involved in carrying out the necessary analysis of resources and requirements can come as something of a shock. The skills demanded are those of the statistician rather than the welfare officer. People must be counted and grouped and their likely behaviour projected on bar charts and graphs. The flow of human resources through the business, rather than the characteristics of individual employees, is what concerns the human resource planner.

What is Involved?

1. Assessing Demand

It is easy to assume that human resource planning is all about the future. In fact, during the initial stages of setting up a plan, and at regular intervals once it is being implemented, analysis of the present situation is vital. Only once those involved have a clear view of how things work now, and how many people are needed to get things done at the current level of output, can realistic plans be drawn up. You may need to become expert in a number of areas.

Organization design. As we saw in Chapter One, there is no such thing as a perfect organization design. But there are some very imperfect, or inappropriate ones. Before anyone starts working out how many people and with what skills will be needed in future, it is as well to make sure that they are not being wasted or frustrated at present in a badly designed organization. Some of the questions you may need to ask or help to answer will include:

- is the overall structure designed to help achieve the organization's goals? Is it flexible enough to accommodate changing priorities?
- does each part have its own clearly identifiable part to play in the achievement of overall objectives – or is there some overlap and duplication of effort?
- are there enough levels of management and supervision, or too many?
- is it clear who has authority over whom – and for what? Are there appropriate channels for communicating between one function and another?

These are not questions which can be answered by personnel alone. But a professional personnel manager, who has studied the various forms of organization design and who understands the culture of his or her own organization, will be well qualified to help the chief executive to work out the answers. If changes are needed, it will be better to identify them now, and to plan for the new structure rather than the old.

Job design. Just as a badly designed organization can thwart attempts to achieve planned goals, so badly designed jobs can mean a waste of human resources. If you have ever had to carry out tasks which you felt were pointless, you will know how frustrating this can be. Asking people to do things which do not contribute, clearly and directly, to the achievement of the organization's objectives, is poor use of human resources. Asking them to use outdated working methods or obsolete equipment is also poor use of their skills.

A review of job design will involve observing and analysing each job to check that it is designed to enable the job holder to work swiftly and effectively to achieve their results. It is

Using outdated working methods . . .

important to make sure that time and effort is not wasted
in badly planned work layouts or travel itineraries, poorly
coordinated handover of work, unnecessary checking and
waiting time, and so on.

To carry out such a review, you will need

- training in method study, job analysis and job design;
- a questioning and analytical approach;
- the self-confidence to challenge accepted methods and ideas;
- the persuasive powers to convince others of the value of
  your proposals.

Line management will need to be convinced that any changes
which you recommend will be more efficient – i.e. will make
better use of resources – and/or more effective – i.e. will
produce a better end result. Employees will need to be
convinced that proposed new methods will be no harder
or less safe than the old, and that they will not be affected
financially by the change. Both groups will want to know
how long it will take to make the change, and what the
implications are in terms of retraining, new equipment and
systems.

Only when all concerned are satisfied that the change is
workable will you be able to go ahead and plan on the basis
of the anticipated improved use of human resources.

Assessing results. Even if there are no obvious deficiencies in organization or job design, your workforce may still be under-used. Before you start planning for the future, it is wise to look closely at what is being achieved now. At worst, it will give you a basis for calculating how many people will be needed to produce a given level of output in future. At best, it will highlight areas where output is low or declining and where remedial action – in the form of better training, improved incentives or revised working methods – is needed.

This will involve careful analysis of all the relevant indicators of productivity. If they are not available from your finance department, you may find yourself trying to assess such things as the *per capita* (per head) sales of the entire workforce. This will mean applying formulae to figures in the company accounts. Other relevant calculations could include

- sales per hour worked (sales staff only)
- units produced per hour worked (production staff)
- calls per hour (telephonists)
- letters per hour (typists).

In isolation they will tell you very little. Compared over time, or between sections or with other companies, they can highlight issues requiring attention.

You may also need to present or analyse information about staff numbers. How does the ratio of 'support' to 'front line' staff look? Is it getting higher, or lower? If it's higher, have you got too many people sitting in head office pushing pieces of paper about – or too few out at the 'sharp end', making and selling your product or service? What about the management to staff ratio? Have you got 'too many chiefs and not enough Indians' – or vice versa? Lack of attention to these ratios can lead to unnecessarily high payroll costs and can demotivate the people who really make money for the business.

Answering such questions will take time, especially if you have to start from scratch gathering productivity data. It also requires a head for figures and the ability to make sense of financial information. To play a useful role in this aspect of human resource planning, you will need to get to grips with the performance data produced by and for line management, and perhaps ask for more or different information to enable a sensible analysis to be made.

Calculating demand. Once you know how much each employee can produce in an hour, it should be relatively easy to calculate how many employee hours will be needed to produce a given level of output in future. The calculation will be a little more complicated if changes in organization or job design are to be introduced during the period – but as long as the assumptions made about improvements in output are clearly recorded it will be possible to monitor and adjust as necessary.

This of course presupposes that the required level of output has been accurately identified – in the corporate plan – and that it will not suddenly change during the period over which human resources are being planned. In practice, the corporate planning process tends to be one of constant revision and adjustment as the future unfolds, and so does human resource planning.

If you are the kind of person who likes everything 'cut and dried', you may find this frustrating. If, on the other hand, you revel in the need to strive for ever increasing accuracy while tolerating the imperfections of an uncertain world, you could find you have a useful contribution to make here.

2. Assessing Supply

In Chapter Two we highlighted the importance of keeping accurate and up-to-date records, in a form which lends itself to analysis by groups of employee. The statistics which you produce will play a vital role in helping to predict the future availability of human resources.

Among the key questions which are likely to arise are:

- how many of the people who are with us now are likely to be with us, in the same jobs, in two years' time?

    Your ability to analyse labour turnover, retirements, promotions and transfers will be the key here, but you will also need to take account of any proposed changes in organization or job design, and/or external factors, which may alter the pattern for the future;

- up to now, we've always assumed an average absence rate of seven days per person per year. Is this likely to change?

  To answer this you will need absence statistics for enough years to establish a trend, an analysis of the most frequently occurring reasons for absence, and an intelligent guess as to whether rates are likely to continue on the present trend;

- our corporate plan calls for a 20 per cent increase in output. Even allowing for productivity improvements, this is going to mean a 12 per cent increase in the number of employee hours we need in skilled areas. Is the current throughput from our training scheme enough to cope with this?

  You will not be able to respond unless you have adequate data on the quantity and quality of trainees, and can match their projected training completion dates against the revised production schedules;

- at the moment our main source of supply for management posts is our graduate training scheme. Are we likely to be able to continue to recruit in the same numbers and from the same degree disciplines as we do at present? If we cannot, what alternatives should we be considering?

  Answering this question, and others about the availability of external recruits, will take you into a whole new area of labour market analysis. Most line managers will expect their personnel specialists to have a sound understanding of employment trends generally. They will also expect you to be well-informed about local trends, including the output from local schools, the availability of part-time workers, travel to work patterns, major changes in the number or composition of the local population, and the activities of those with whom you compete for human resources.

3. Reconciling Demand and Supply

Wherever the answers to questions such as those above indicate that there may not be enough people, or people with the right skills, to meet demand, you will need to formulate a recruitment plan. As we shall see in Chapter Four, this may not mean external recruitment. It could be that the development and transfer of existing employees will help to make good at least some of the deficit.

Wherever the answers indicate that there are too many people, or people with the wrong skills, you will need to formulate a termination plan. While this may involve redundancy and/or retirement arrangements to reduce the overall numbers employed, it may also include a transfer plan to enable those who are surplus to requirements in one part of the organization to be redeployed to another part where their skills can be developed and used.

In later chapters we will examine in more detail what is involved in both recruitment and termination. Here, it is enough to note that work on drawing up both types of plan requires careful attention to detail and constant questioning of the premises on which the plans are based.

Suppose, for example, that the corporate plan does call for a 20 per cent increase in output. If customer demand for the product actually increases only by 12 per cent, and if productivity gains produce a 12 per cent saving rather than eight per cent as anticipated, the 12 per cent increase in employee numbers for which you have planned will no longer be required. In an ideal world, you would be informed of this in good time, so that you did not waste your own or the candidates' time recruiting unwanted labour.

Unfortunately, the marketing director may not think through the manpower implications of all this when he or she is coming to terms with the need to revise the forecast. So, unless you are constantly in tune with what is happening in other parts of the business, you could find that you are the one who is out of step.

4. Monitoring the Plan

Even if you are not directly involved in drawing up your organization's human resource plan, you may well find you are called upon to help monitor its implementation. You may, for instance, be asked to provide a periodic 'headcount against establishment'. This will enable top management to assess whether the number of people in each department is as anticipated. Per capita employment costs, again on a departmental basis, may also be required regularly.

The labour turnover statistics produced as a basis for planning will need to be updated, probably monthly, to make sure there are no sudden deviations which would invalidate the assumptions on which the plan was based. Progress towards target recruitment for each category of employee, must also be kept under review. This may mean you are asked to count recent and forthcoming joiners and to calculate any shortfall. If there is a termination plan, again progress will need to be reported regularly.

Who does What?

Human resource planning is a complex task. It is certainly not one that should be attempted single-handed. Few of the sample questions posed in this chapter can be answered in the peace and tranquillity of the personnel department. Most involve going out to observe and ask questions – of line management and employees generally – to establish what is happening now and what is likely to happen in the future.

This is especially true during the initial stages of drawing up the plan. Personnel can 'ask the right questions' to help line management assess their future demand for particular categories of employee. But the plan itself will only be as sound as the line management information on which it is based. If the corporate plan is vague or unrealistic, or if data about current staff usage is inaccurate, the most sophisticated personnel system will not be able to compensate.

The personnel department can take the lead in examining the external issues which will affect the supply of new recruits. The generalized warnings of a 'demographic time bomb' or other such dire press predictions, must be translated into *specifics* for your organization.

One of the best ways to develop an insight into what is happening in your local labour market is to take part in the activities of your local IPM branch. This will bring you into contact with other personnel practitioners who are operating in the same area and who will help to keep you in touch with local issues. You can also foster contacts with the Jobcentre manager, the careers staff at local schools and the Local Education Authority Careers office, and with relevant local government officials who can keep you informed of changes affecting the local population.

The other main contribution which the personnel department will be expected to make is the provision of the relevant employment statistics – such as employee numbers, absence rates, labour turnover, age profiles and employment costs.

In smaller and less complex organizations, or those where the pace of change is generally slower, senior personnel and line managers may be able to draw up a sensible 'pencil and paper' plan without the need for further specialist help. This will simply list anticipated demand and internal supply for each employment category for each month or quarter, and cross-refer to an appropriately phased recruitment and/or termination/transfer plan.

If, however, a more complex statistical approach is called for, specialist help will be required. It will be worth investing in a trained statistician or econometrician, who can interpret historical data and design a computerized 'model' of the organization. He or she will then be able to feed in alternative sets of data and report their effects. This in turn will enable top management to consider a range of possible future situations or 'scenarios' and to decide how best to respond.

Who can Help?

In this chapter we have done no more than provide a glimpse of the complexities of human resource planning. If you are charged with responsibility in this area, you will need a much more in-depth understanding of what is involved.

Your best sources are:

Books

For an overview and some practical guidance

Practical Manpower Planning, Fourth edition, John Bramham, IPM, 1988.
and
Human Resource Planning, John Bramham, IPM, 1989.

For more detailed understanding of some of the underlying issues

   The Missing Workforce: Managing absenteeism, Andrew Sargent, IPM, 1989.
and
   Job Analysis: A practical guide for managers, M Pearn and R Kandola, IPM, 1988.
and
   Labour Turnover, Barrie Pettman (ed), Gower, 1974.

Other

As we have seen, the human resource plan must be based on careful analysis of organization and job design and presupposes the existence of a clear and realistic corporate plan. To help your top management get these things into sharper focus, and to begin to see the human resource implications of their existing approach, you may find that a management consultant, skilled in analytical and diagnostic work, will help you to get onto the right track. He or she may be able to ask more searching and challenging questions, and be less bogged down by shared assumptions, based on 'the way we've always done things', than members of the personnel department could.

One organization which specializes in the development of human resource planning models is the Institute of Manpower Studies. You can contact them at the University of Sussex, telephone number 0273 686751.

Chapter Four

Recruitment and Selection

Introduction

Effective recruitment and selection are the keys to getting the right people in the right place at the right time. They also form a major area of activity for most personnel departments. To see them as just one task is, however, an over-simplification. The process divides into two main areas:

- recruitment – that is attracting a field of suitably qualified candidates;
- selection – that is predicting which candidate(s) will make the most appropriate contribution to the job and the organization – now and in the future.

Both recruitment and selection in turn comprise many different tasks, which are usually shared out between members of the personnel team and line managers.

What is Involved?

Personnel Requisitions

The first task is to make sure a vacancy really exists. Is the position one which will continue to feature in the organization's human resource plan (see Chapter Three)? Or is it one which is due to be phased out anyway?

Even if it is included in the plan, it may still be appropriate to ask the relevant line manager to 'make the case' for recruitment – perhaps using a personnel requisition form approved by their own boss. This will provide an opportunity to review the work of the department as a whole, and to consider whether the duties of the vacant position can be reallocated between other employees, to provide more variety for them and/or to reduce costs for the organization.

A senior member of the personnel team – perhaps the personnel director – may set up such a system to help the board to control employee costs. He or she may also be one of the people with authority to approve recruitment. More junior personnel people may become involved once the requisition has been approved. Only then will they be authorized to start looking for a means of filling the vacancy.

Job Descriptions

The next task is to find out as much as possible about the vacancy. Some personnel departments make a practice of interviewing everyone who resigns from the organization. These *exit interviews* can be a valuable way of discovering what a job involves – and what satisfactions and frustrations it offers.

In addition, a carefully drawn up job description can provide much of the information that will be needed in deciding where and who to recruit. Although the present job holder(s), if there is one, and their immediate boss, are best placed to provide accurate information about what the job entails, the personnel department often contributes by:

- designing an appropriate pro forma for drawing up a job description;
- giving advice to line managers on how to complete the job description;
- providing a specialist job analysis service whereby a trained member of the personnel team will observe and interview job holders and use this as the basis for compiling a job description.

Many personnel departments build up a library of job descriptions, based on a standard format. If your organization has such a system, you may be involved in periodic audits to make sure that the descriptions held are up to date. In any case, before using an existing job description for recruitment it is good practice to check that it still gives an accurate picture of the job.

Personnel Specifications

The next key task in recruitment is that of drawing up a personnel specification, that is a description of what someone will need to bring with them by way of abilities and motivation if they are to do the job successfully. Again, this is an area for line management involvement, as the manager concerned is likely to have some ideas about the knowledge and skills required to do the job. The personnel department can contribute in a number of ways:

- by helping line managers to think through, systematically and objectively, exactly what they *do* need of the person recruited. In many organizations, it will still be necessary to remind line managers not to assume that members of a particular race, gender or marital group will be either particularly suitable or particularly unsuitable. The Sex Discrimination and Race Relations Acts explicitly forbid employers *directly* discriminating in this way.

   It may also be necessary to stop them discriminating *indirectly* by setting up unjustifiable requirements which will tend to exclude members of a particular group. You could find yourself battling with a line manager who insists that complete geographical mobility (a requirement which could tend to exclude more married than single people) is essential, when in fact the work will largely be concentrated in one particular location. Or you may need to dissuade someone from the view that at least five years' experience is required – but anyone over 25 will be too old. Although there is no law against age discrimination, by setting up this particular combination of requirements, any women who have been away from the labour market for a few years in their early twenties will be excluded. Unless you can show that both requirements are justified – that is, the job cannot be done effectively without them – you may be discriminating indirectly against women with young families.

   Helping a manager to arrive at an objective and usable specification can be a challenging task. Most of us have deep-rooted assumptions about the 'type' of person we can see doing a particular kind of work. Often, we will see this in terms of gender, race, personality and a particular collection of educational qualifications and work experience. In reality though, these things are a lot less effective as a guide to successful performance than a person's basic abilities and their willingness to apply, or learn to apply, these to the job. If you are to make a professional contribution to your organization's recruitment activity, you will need to be able to persuade line managers of this;

- by conducting a systematic analysis of the attributes (selection criteria) which are likely to lead to successful performance in the job. Some organizations now use computer packages to help them focus on the criteria for success. Existing job holders, their bosses and perhaps a personnel specialist are required to respond to a series of questions about the most important and most frequently occurring components of the job. The computer analyses their responses to highlight the underlying abilities, competences or 'dimensions' required. Some packages then go on to suggest which dimensions can be assessed at interview – and what questions should be asked to assess them.

Other organizations approach the identification of selection criteria via an in-depth questionnaire and interview programme with existing job holders. This approach is most often used where there are large numbers of people doing similar, but relatively complex and important jobs. For instance, one company used it to help them select managers for their chain of public houses at a time when high labour turnover and poor trading results suggested that more traditional methods were failing to identify the right people for the jobs. Statistical analysis of the things which successful managers had in common helped to produce a more realistic specification. Further analysis of the things which had attracted those managers to the company, and of the reasons why they stayed, also led to a rethink of the brewery's recruitment advertising.

As you can see, the production of a personnel specification can be a very sophisticated process. Before you get involved, you will need special training so that you understand how to use each method, and how to avoid designing a specification which discriminates unfairly against particular sections of the population.

Recruitment Methods

In many organizations, top management take the view that it is better to promote from within wherever possible. If that is the case in your company, the choice of recruitment method has been made for you. If the position to be filled is above the entry grade, the personnel department will be required either to circulate details of the vacancy, perhaps by posting them on noticeboards or advertising them in the house magazine, or to draw up a list of candidates on the basis of employee records.

In the interests of ensuring that *everyone* has an equal opportunity to be considered, the first of these methods is generally preferable. Unless your organization's personnel information system is 100 per cent accurate in every detail, and your personnel specification so tight that only a very small number are eligible for consideration, the second method could lead to potentially suitable people being overlooked. If the invitation to apply is thrown open to everyone, then even those who have acquired the necessary abilities away from their present jobs can be considered.

Whichever method is used to identify internal candidates for the position, the selection process will follow a similar pattern to that for external recruitment – discussed next.

Where it is not possible to recruit from inside the organization in this way, someone in the personnel department will be charged with the task of 'going outside'. Precisely *where* outside will depend on the nature of the vacancy, the speed with which it must be filled, the size of the advertising budget, and company policy.

Some companies automatically place senior vacancies in the hands of a management consultant – especially if the resources and/or level of seniority of those in the personnel department mean it would be impracticable for them to get too heavily involved. Some always insist on low cost methods – the Jobcentre or an advertisement in the shop or office window or at the factory gate – especially for junior/unskilled employees. For others, the preferred route is advertising in the local, regional or national press or trade or professional journals depending upon the vacancy.

If you become involved in recruitment, you will soon begin to formulate your own picture of which methods/publications seem to produce the best results for particular types of vacancy. Systematic monitoring of this, rather than vague general impressions, will mean that you can point out to the manager who demands an 'Ad in the Standard', that last time you needed someone in Croydon you got a much better response from the Advertiser.

Writing advertisements may sound like one of the more glamourous parts of the work of the personnel department. This is not always true. In large organizations you will often find that advertising has been standardized and must be presented in a certain way to conform to the organization's corporate image. Often this will be done by a professional advertising agency, rather than personnel staff.

Advertising can also be very repetitive. There are not all

that many different ways of wrapping up your requirement for a part-time cleaner. And with a limited budget, and many vacancies best filled locally, your visions of seeing your name in print in the 'Situations Vacant' pages of a national newspaper could be a long time materializing.

Nevertheless, helping line managers to express, clearly and invitingly, the demands that the job will make, and the rewards that it offers, is a real challenge. Your ability to interpret both the job description and the personnel specification, and to convey these concisely to an appropriate audience are the key skills here. Once you have attracted your field of candidates, the next task is to decide how best to select.

Application Forms

Application forms are among the most familiar of personnel department documents. Almost everyone in the department is likely to handle them at some stage, see Figure 3 on page 56. In more complex organizations you may find several different forms which are used for different categories of employee.

Although they may be commonplace within the department, it must be remembered that application forms contain much confidential information. The very fact that someone has applied to your organization could be damaging if their present employer got to hear of it. And if the form contains information about previous or present salaries, reasons for leaving particular jobs, medical information and the like, any breach of confidentiality would reflect very badly on the professionalism of the personnel department.

Interviews

When it comes to deciding which applicant most closely matches their personnel specification, most organizations still place a great deal of reliance on the interview. All members of the personnel team are likely to have some contact with those attending for interview – whether it be the secretary or clerical assistant who writes or telephones to invite candidates to attend, the receptionist who greets them when they arrive, the personnel officer/recruitment specialist

Figure 3
Application Forms

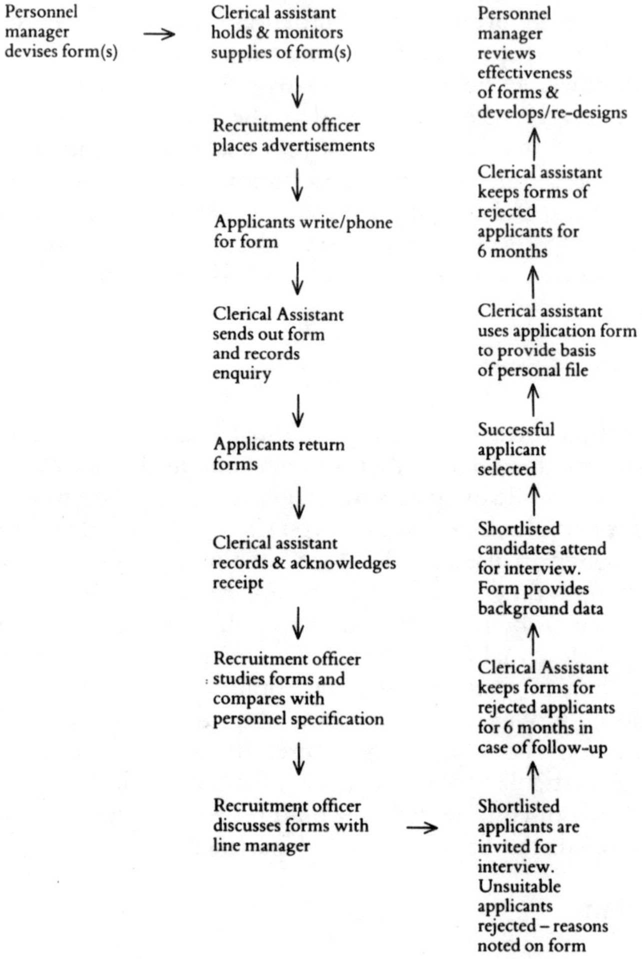

Personnel manager devises form(s) → Clerical assistant holds & monitors supplies of form(s)

↓

Recruitment officer places advertisements

↓

Applicants write/phone for form

↓

Clerical Assistant sends out form and records enquiry

↓

Applicants return forms

↓

Clerical assistant records & acknowledges receipt

↓

Recruitment officer studies forms and compares with personnel specification

↓

Recruitment officer discusses forms with line manager →

Personnel manager reviews effectiveness of forms & develops/re-designs

↑

Clerical assistant keeps forms of rejected applicants for 6 months

↑

Clerical assistant uses application form to provide basis of personal file

↑

Successful applicant selected

↑

Shortlisted candidates attend for interview. Form provides background data

↑

Clerical Assistant keeps forms for rejected applicants for 6 months in case of follow-up

↑

Shortlisted applicants are invited for interview. Unsuitable applicants rejected – reasons noted on form

who carries out preliminary interviews, or the personnel manager who actually makes the offer of employment.

Because interviews are such a regular feature of life in the personnel department, it is easy to forget that for the candidates they may be very stressful occasions. Whatever your level of involvement with those attending for interview, it is important to make them feel welcome and to help them relax. Remember, too, that the impressions gained during their visit may make a difference to whether the selected candidate accepts or rejects your offer of employment. Take the opportunity to let them see what your organization is really like, so that they take away an accurate picture of what it would be like to work there.

If you are involved in conducting interviews yourself, you will of course need training in the specialist skills which this requires. Establishing the right atmosphere, and asking the right questions to enable the candidate to provide accurate and relevant information about his or her suitability, calls for considerable skill.

However good you are at talking to people, to be a successful interviewer, you will need more. You will need to be able to

- ask for specific examples, and seek out 'contrary evidence' to enable you to gain a balanced picture of how the candidate usually behaves. This will be of far more value than mere general impressions;
- probe, gently but deeply, so that you never settle for the superficial;
- keep your own personal prejudices firmly in check. If they are to be of value to your organization, your conclusions must be based on careful analysis of the candidate's ability to meet the demands which the job will make – not your own likes and dislikes. While 'gut feel' or instinct *may* play a part, your assessment must stem from a systematic and objective appraisal of what the candidate can and can't do, set against the requirements laid out in your personnel specification.

In most organizations, recruitment decisions are shared between personnel and line management. The personnel team may decide who to shortlist, but the final decision about who to appoint will either be shared or left to the line manager. Sometimes personnel specialists conduct a preliminary interview, to explore the non-technical aspects of the candidate's suitability. Those who are found to lack the motivation to succeed, or to conform to the organization's requirements for honesty, integrity, punctuality and attendance, may be screened out at this stage.

The relevant line manager will then conduct a second interview, to probe ability to do the job to the required standard. Either or both interviewers may also try to establish whether the candidate is likely to develop beyond the job which is immediately available, and make a long term contribution to the business.

Alternatively, particularly for more senior posts, it may be more cost effective for a joint personnel/line management interview to be held. In this case, the personnel representative will often find themselves acting as chairperson, trying to make sure that the other people involved ask their questions in a logical sequence, don't overlap, and don't confuse the candidates.

Either way, the personnel professional will want to make sure that the decisions reached are well-founded, and that no unfair discrimination has taken place. As with helping line managers to draw up the personnel specification, you may encounter some who are inclined to let their prejudices show. They will argue that 'she' won't work the extra hours that the job demands – because of course she has domestic responsibilities. Or that clients won't feel at ease with 'him' (a member of an ethnic minority).

The personnel specialist must question these assumptions, and help others to consider each candidate as an individual, not as a member of a particular sex or race. He or she should encourage managers to analyse the skills which candidates have – rather than whether they come from the same background as previous job holders and/or the rest of the employees. Positive discrimination – that is selecting someone *because* they are black/female/married, etc. – is illegal. But turning someone down because, for example, their organizational skills were acquired running a parent-teachers' association or a community group rather than in paid employment, is both short-sighted and potentially discriminatory.

Becoming a truly effective interviewer, one who can help line managers to predict accurately and fairly who will contribute positively to the future of the organization, is one of the key challenges you will face if you work in a personnel department. The skill and concentrated effort you will need,

- to question,
- to listen,
- to show sincere interest,
- to weigh up objectively,

even when you're seeing the sixth or seventh candidate that day – should not be underestimated.

The compensation lies in meeting new people each day, and in having the chance to make a really positive contribution to the future success of your organization.

Tests

An increasing number of employers recognize that the interview alone is not necessarily the best way to predict who will succeed in a job. Tests, of knowledge, skill, the aptitude to learn, basic intelligence or personality, play an important part in many selection procedures.

The personnel specialist must be in a position to advise on the use (and abuse) of such tests. Inappropriate tests, sloppily administered or interpreted by those untrained in their use, can do untold damage. Candidates may be discriminated against unfairly, and poor selection decisions made, unless someone with the necessary knowledge and skill

- works out what abilities need to be tested;
- identifies a test which measures those abilities with a reasonable degree of reliability (that is, gives constant results when repeated) and validity (that is, relates to performance in the job);
- assesses what score in the test should be taken as an indication that someone is unlikely to succeed in the job;
- adminsters the test, under standardized conditions (that is, giving the same amount of time, the same instructions, the same equipment, the same environment, for all candidates);
- scores the test, using appropriate standards;

- interprets the test result;
- feeds back the results – to selectors and, where appropriate, candidates.

Sometimes this work will be shared between members of the personnel team. The personnel manager may be directly involved in most aspects, and will certainly be the one who influences company policy on whether or not tests are to be used. The administration and scoring of the tests may however be delegated to more junior members of the team. All involved must of course be trained by one of the testing bodies approved by the British Psychological Society.

Because many people worry even more about tests than about attending for interviews, personnel staff need to be especially sensitive to this. Even if you are not directly involved in administering or interpreting the test, you will need to make sure you do nothing to heighten the candidates' apprehension. You must also be careful not to give away anything about what the test requires or means. Most tests only work when candidates are unfamiliar with their contents. If you start telling candidates, or your friends and relations, about the test questions, you will severely reduce its value.

Similarly, if you divulge test scores to those not authorized to have them, you could damage the successful candidate's chances of doing well in their new job. This is because test scores are usually only one of the factors upon which selection decisions are based. Imagine how the new recruit whose score on a particular test happened to be a bit borderline would fare if news of this got out. Everyone would be expecting this to be a weak area. They may be right – such prophecies are often self-fulfilling.

Assessment Centres

Because candidates who are good talkers and experienced test-sitters do not always turn out to be good at the jobs for which they are recruited, some organizations now go a step further. They use a series of exercises or activities to simulate key parts of the job itself. That way, the recruiters can observe how candidates actually *do* perform.

Assessment centres, as these activities are called, bring

together groups of candidates and selectors, sometimes for periods of 48 hours or more. Each candidate will perform some of the exercises alone – giving a presentation, for example, or sorting out the priorities in a mock 'in-tray'. They will also work with other candidates, to solve problems or agree a plan of action, or simply to discuss ideas. By watching them at work on a variety of different tasks, the selectors can obtain a more accurate assessment of their capabilities.

The exercises used must be designed to reflect the demands which the job itself will make. The selectors must be trained in what to look for and how to assess it. Skilled staff within the personnel department can help with both these aspects, as well as providing the considerable administrative back-up which is needed to get all the candidates and selectors to the right place at the right time, with the right information and associated paperwork.

Medicals

Physical and/or mental fitness can sometimes be crucial in determining whether or not a particular candidate should be selected. It is in no-one's interest for employees to be placed in situations which are beyond their capabilities.

Company policy will dictate whether a satisfactory medical report is essential for all positions, or only for specified jobs. Personnel staff will need to liaise with the company medical centre or occupational health unit, if there is one, or with the candidate's own GP if there isn't. The procedure should take full account of the candidate's legal right to see any information supplied by their doctor.

The personnel department will also need to monitor the organization's quota of registered disabled employees. All organizations which employ more than 20 people must employ a minimum of three per cent registered disabled – unless they have been granted exemption. The personnel department can also take positive action to take advantage of the grants and other forms of help which are available to encourage the employment of the disabled.

References

Some organizations take the view that their selection procedures are rigorous enough to ensure that those chosen will be suitable employees. Others believe that the additional insight to be gained from speaking or writing to the candidate's previous employers, is important.

Whether or not your personnel department makes a practice of contacting previous employers – sending them a standard form to complete or asking for more general comments, you are likely to be on the receiving end of requests for references from other employers. These may be in writing, over the telephone or, occasionally, face-to-face.

Great care must be taken when giving references. If you carelessly muddle up one Mr A B Sykes – who was dismissed for dishonesty – with another Mr A B Sykes – who was a model employee, the employer who relies on the information you supply and offers a job to the first Mr Sykes, may have a legal claim against you. Similarly, if you say something in a reference which you cannot substantiate, and which damages the reputation of your employee, he or she may sue you.

Although references will usually be checked by a senior member of the personnel team, the job of sorting out the answers to the questions asked, often falls to more junior staff. Take particular care with telephone references. You can never be sure who is on the other end of the line – unless you ask if you can call them back, and check their number. Rather than entering into a discussion over the phone, it is usually safer just to confirm that the person concerned was employed by you between the dates claimed – and to ask for any other information to be requested in writing.

(Similar caution should be exercised when dealing with requests for information from finance companies, banks, building societies, and people claiming to be relatives or friends of members of your staff. You should *never* divulge information about salaries, conditions of employment, or addresses or telephone numbers, without the express permission of the person concerned.)

Selection Follow-up

Before a final decision is made, everything that is known about each candidate must be weighed carefully against the personnel specification. Personnel specialists can help line managers to interpret the information they have gathered, and to pinpoint each candidate's strengths and weaknesses. Occasionally, the personnel specialist may insist that a particular candidate be excluded from further consideration because of some fundamental concern. But in most organizations the final decision about which candidate will be offered the post will rest with the line manager.

The personnel department's involvement does not end here, though. The unsuccessful candidates must be informed that they have not been selected. They are bound to feel some disappointment. A curt little note saying: 'Sorry, you weren't good enough', will only add to their sense of failure. A little thought given to personalizing 'standard' rejection letters can provide some positive public relations for your company. The speed with which such letters are sent may also influence candidates' view.

Speed is also of the essence when making an offer to the chosen candidate. If they have been looking for a job, they may have other offers they are considering. A quick response – perhaps an evening telephone call from the personnel manager – will make your organization special.

The content of the offer will be a matter for discussion between personnel and line management. The rate of pay must be decided, probably by reference to established scales – see Chapter Seven. Other terms and conditions of employment, holiday entitlements, sick pay arrangements, pension scheme details, company car information and relocation package (if applicable), must all be laid out in the offer letter. Unless the chosen candidate can see what you are offering, and is attracted by it, you still risk losing your new recruit.

Effective follow-up also means that

- if no reply is received, someone must make contact with the candidate to find out why;

- once a start date has been agreed, someone must set up a personal record, someone must notify the payroll department, the pensions department (if there is one) and the line manager;
- someone must arrange for the newcomer to be greeted on arrival on their first morning, to be taken to their department and introduced, to be given a basic introduction to the company and to what is expected of them;
- someone must make sure that all the legal requirements associated with what is now a legally binding agreement are fulfilled. A contract of employment, covering all the points specified in the Employment Protection (Consolidation) Act, 1978, must be drawn up and should be signed by a representative of the company (usually the personnel manager), and the employee;
- someone must set up and implement an appropriate *validation* procedure, once the new recruit has settled in. The chosen candidate's actual performance in the job should be compared with the predictions of performance made during selection, perhaps by comparing current performance ratings (see Chapter Six), with test scores or assessment centre predictions and interview ratings. If those candidates who are expected to perform well in particular aspects of the job do so, you can have some confidence in the predictive value of your selection procedure. If they don't, it may be necessary to take a fresh look at the procedure, to try to identify which parts are failing.

In all these cases, that 'someone' is likely to be a member of the personnel team. In larger organizations, the work will be split. But whatever the size of your organization, none of it can be omitted. Remember, too, that in this chapter we have worked through the recruitment and selection process as though you had only one vacancy to fill. The reality, for all but the smallest, most stable organizations, will be that all of these activities are going on, all the time, for tens, or even hundreds, of jobs, every month. In large retail or catering companies, for example, where labour turnover is often high, the task of entering the personal details of all new starters on the computerized personnel information system can take several hours each week.

Who Does What?

In your personnel department, you may find that there is a recruitment officer or a team of people specializing in recruitment. Even so, you will find it hard to avoid all involvement in recruitment and selection – if only because so many of the incoming telephone calls in most personnel departments are to do with vacancies which have been advertised or with people applying 'on spec'.

In particular, line managers will expect their personnel department to have a smooth and efficient administration system so that

- requisitions are acted on;
- advertisements are placed promptly, in appropriate places and at appropriate cost;
- potential candidates receive application forms, invitations to interviews, tests, etc., promptly and accompanied by polite and helpful letters;
- unsuccessful candidates are notified, promptly and politely;
- interview, test and assessment centre timings, venues, accommodation and travel arrangements, and so forth, are efficiently managed;
- medicals are arranged and references are taken up in a speedy and professional manner;
- appropriately worded offer letters are sent promptly and are followed up;
- appropriate arrangements are made for welcoming the newcomer and introducing him or her to the organization;
- contracts of employment are issued and other documents handled in accordance with legal requirements;
- some assessment is made of the accuracy of selection predictions.

The personnel department, in turn, needs to work with line managers to ensure

- job descriptions and realistic, unbiased personnel specifications are available;
- application form screening, tests, interviews and assessment centres are conducted in a way which ensures that candidates are fairly treated and that the relevant indicators of their suitability/unsuitability are properly examined;
- selection decisions are made only with regard to objective, job-related selection criteria – not prejudice or personal bias;
- pay and conditions offered to new recruits are appropriate in relation to existing members of the team they are joining, and/or the rest of the organization;
- the new recruit receives a positive introduction to his or her new job – and quickly becomes a competent member of a settled team.

Of course not all these activities will necessarily be handled through head office personnel departments. Where line managers are scattered across the country or the continent, for example, it would be wasteful and time consuming for recruitment documentation to be sent back and forth to the central personnel department. In some cases, a local or regional personnel office may handle the personnel end of recruitment. In others, it will be more cost effective for line managers to be trained to take on more of their own recruitment. In such cases, central personnel may simply ensure that requisitions are authorized, co-ordinate the placing of advertisements and issue contracts of employment – leaving the manager on the spot to deal with the rest.

Who Can Help?

If you are new to personnel and are working without the support of an established personnel department, you must make sure you are equipped with the right knowledge and skills before you start. It is unfair to your organization, your applicants and yourself, to dabble in this area without a knowledge of the law relating to recruitment and selection and some skill in handling the procedures involved.

Books

Your knowledge of the law can come from reading:

Essentials of Employment Law, Third edition, David Lewis, IPM, 1990.

Contracts at Work, Erich Suter, IPM, 1982.

The Employment Law Checklist, Fourth edition, Erich Suter, IPM, 1990.

You will find a general overview of recruitment and selection in

Success in Management: Personnel, Third edition, Penny Hackett, John Murray, 1990.

or

Recruitment and Selection, Fifth edition, Philip Plumbley, IPM, 1991.

and advice on specific aspects in

Interviews: Skills and Strategy, John Courtis, IPM, 1988.

Psychological Testing: A practical guide to aptitude and other tests, John Toplis, Vic Dulewicz and Clive Fletcher, IPM, 1987.

A Good Start: Effective employee induction, Second edition, Alan Fowler, IPM, 1990.

Courses

The skills involved in designing and implementing recruitment and selection procedures can only come from a combination of practice and constructive feedback. If you can't manage the full IPM professional education programme (see Chapter Ten), you should at least attend one or more of the reputable short courses which are available. The Institute offer such courses regularly, as do the Staff Management Association and Croner Conferences.

Consultants

If you need help with part of the recruitment and selection process, there is no shortage of agencies and consultants who (for a fee), will help you to do anything from placing an advertisement to designing an assessment centre.

For advice on selecting a consultant, you can contact the IPM Personnel Consultancy Assignment Service, telephone number 081 946 9100. They will offer you access to the professional expertise of IPM member consultants.

Legal Advice

If you have particular concerns about recruiting the disabled, your local Disablement Resettlement Officer can be contacted through the Department of Employment.

If you are worried about equal opportunities, the Equal Opportunities Commission can provide detailed guidance on issues relating to sex and marital status. They will send you information and case law examples.

Similarly, the Commission for Racial Equality will help with queries relating to race. Alternatively, the Department of Employment Race Relations Advisory Service is available to help you to educate yourself and your colleagues, and to get you thinking positively about equal opportunities.

Legal advice on specific issues can be obtained through the IPM Employment Law Advisory Service, which is free to members of the Institute. The Industrial Society or Croner Call may also be able to help.

More generally, the manager of your local Jobcentre can often be a mine of useful information and guidance – on everything from competitive pay rates to government employment programmes.

Chapter Five

Training and Development

Introduction

When people with the potential to become effective employees have been recruited, the next task for the personnel department is to make sure they have the chance to realize that potential. This is where training and development come in.

Training helps people to acquire the knowledge and skills needed for successful performance of their present jobs. But neither people nor jobs stand still for very long. All organizations need people who can help to move the business forward, and who will be able to take on more senior responsibilities in the future. This is the 'development' angle.

Both training and development are vital to business success. The difficulties which arise when training has not been done, or not been done effectively, are all too obvious. The sales assistant who cannot answer your questions about the product you might have bought; the teacher who does not know how to maintain the interest of a class; or, more tragically, the railway worker who does not recognize the danger signals indicating the approach of an oncoming train – are probably not *personally* inadequate. They simply have not been trained.

Less immediately obvious, but equally damaging, are the consequences of lack of development. The elderly director who is getting less and less effective, but who cannot retire – because no-one has the breadth of knowledge and understanding of the business to succeed to the position; the previously successful organization which is no longer quite at the forefront of new business development – because its people are resting on their laurels instead of looking forward; the company which consistently fails to attract as many highly qualified recruits as its competitors – because employees are not given the chance to grow and use their talents to the full: are all suffering from lack of development.

What is Involved?

Just as some people think recruitment is glamourous because it involves interviewing, some think training is glamourous because it involves standing up and making presentations. In fact, that is only a small part of what training is about. It is the work which goes on before and after any 'stand up' training session, and (often) the willingness to abandon such sessions altogether in favour of other more appropriate forms of learning, which makes for real effectiveness in training. The first key task is to work out who needs training, and in what.

1. Analysing Training Needs

The last thing most organizations would want to do is to waste time and money training people in things which are irrelevant to the demands of their jobs – or which they can do already. To avoid this, the personnel manager or, if there is one, the training officer, must find the answers to two main questions – not just once, but for every type of job within the organization.

- What competences do job holders need – that is, what must they be able to do, and to what standard?
- What can each job holder do already?

Neither of these questions can be answered just by sitting thinking. The answer to the first will only come from establishing just what those who do the job well, that is who achieve the right results, actually *do*. An accurate job description, like the one prepared for recruitment purposes (see Chapter Four), can help here. But often it will be necessary to probe behind the tasks themselves, to examine the ingredients which go to make successful performance.

Line managers who have observed people in action on the job will be able to shed some light on this. First-hand observation by the training specialist, or reference to a list of published competences such as those produced for management jobs by the Management Charter Initiative, may also be used.

Take, for example, the job of office manager. To succeed in this job, the main requirement might, at first sight, seem to be 'managerial competence'. But what does that mean? The trainer will need to break this down to establish what particular aspects of managerial competence are most important: planning skills, organizational skills, interpersonal skills, and so on, and what specific knowledge is needed in relation to, for example, company systems, legal requirements, information technology.

So far as the second question is concerned, you are likely to find that the way this is dealt with depends on whether the job holders are newly recruited or established employees. If the former, the selection process should go some way towards identifying what the new recruits can and cannot do. The difference between their present competences and those needed for successful performance in the job is sometimes referred to as the *training gap*.

The size and shape of the training gap will be assessed at interview, and during any assessment centre or testing components of selection. The more closely these simulate the job itself, the easier it will be to assess the gap. If the gap is very wide, a fairly lengthy and detailed training programme may be needed to help them reach the required standard of performance. If it is small, a basic re-orientation, to help them understand specific company systems and procedures may be all that is called for.

To identify the training needs of established employees, many organizations use *performance appraisal*. In Chapter Six you will find a more detailed explanation of what this involves and of the role of personnel specialists in devising and administering such schemes. Here, it is enough for us to note that these regular discussions between job holders and their bosses, highlighting how present performance matches up to what is expected, and how it can be improved further, can provide a very useful input to the identification of training needs.

When it comes to assessing potential for further development, however, performance in job holders' present jobs may not be the best guide. The competences required in more senior posts may differ from those used at present. For this reason, some organizations use assessment centres designed to assess the competences needed in more senior posts. Individual development programmes (perhaps involving secondment to other departments), special projects or attendance at relevant courses, are then designed to enable the successful candidates to fulfil their potential.

Line management involvement in the identification of both training and development needs is essential. Personnel may help to devise the mechanisms to bring this about. They may provide advice and guidance to the line manager who believes the only way to improve the performance of his or her people is to 'Sack the lot and start again!' But the opportunity to observe people at work, to analyse where they are having difficulties, and to identify the underlying causes of these difficulties, is part and parcel of every line manager's responsibility for getting the best from what is usually their most vital resource.

2. Meeting Training Needs

Some managers (and personnel practitioners) assume that any training need which has been identified can only be met by sending people away on expensive courses. This may lead some to shy away from trying to remedy training needs – on the basis that they have neither the time nor the money to send their people away. Others will demand courses for everything – and be bitterly disappointed when their people come back apparently none the wiser for their week at the company training centre, or their month at an expensive business school.

One key role for the personnel or training professional is to explode this myth. Frequent and intensive discussion with line managers may be needed to help them to understand that in many cases, the most effective source of learning for their people is likely to be found within the job itself. This does not mean simply leaving people to 'pick things up the hard way'. It means providing carefully structured experience within the job, with careful instruction and equally careful 'debriefing' to help the job holder reflect on – and thereby consolidate

– learning. Where this cannot be arranged within the daily routine – perhaps because of safety or quality implications – it may nevertheless be possible for line managers to provide the necessary instruction and practice during special training sessions or as part of a carefully designed off-job training programme, see below.

More generally, the personnel department will be expected to give professional advice on how best to meet the needs which have been identified. What combination of on-job instruction, in-house courses, distance learning, technology-based training, project work, coaching, external courses or other methods will best satisfy the identified needs?

3. Clarifying Learning Objectives

'Send Jason on the course that Tracy went on. It did wonders for her . . . it's just what he needs.' Before making the booking, the experienced trainer will ask just one question. 'What precisely do you want Jason to be able to *do* after the course?' If the answer is exactly the same as when the same question was asked about Tracy, and if the course did indeed 'do wonders' for her, it may be sensible to go ahead. But if the answer is different, the course may not be the best solution.

Clarifying learning objectives means coming up with a clear, concise statement of what competences you expect people to have, that is, what you want them to be able to do after they have been trained, and to what standard and within what time-scale you want them to be able to do it. For example:

At the end of their training programme, trainees will be able to wordprocess at least eight one-page letters per hour, without errors and in accordance with the approved house style.

Only when the learning objectives are clear will the trainer be in a position to advise on how best they can be met. If you are to be involved in the training function, you will need to be able to think logically and have the persuasive power to encourage others to think clearly and analytically about the precise objectives they want to meet. Once the desired outcome has been agreed, trainer *and* line manager can begin to think about how best to achieve it.

4. Designing Training Programmes

The credible training specialist will be able to distinguish between the different stages in what is known as the learning cycle. He or she must also realize that different people learn in different ways – and that techniques which are appropriate to build knowledge may not be so appropriate for the development of technical or interpersonal skills.

As well as a thorough understanding of the principles of learning, training calls for an in-depth knowledge of the alternatives available. The resources of the organization must be analysed – to assess the extent to which training needs can be met in-house. Government training schemes and grant facilities must be studied, to see if any or all of the company's training effort might qualify for assistance. Other resources, from the local Training and Enterprise Council (TEC) and the Training Agency to colleges, polytechnics, universities, business schools and consultancies must be examined, so that the trainer can readily identify the best way of meeting specific needs.

If the necessary expertise, time, and other resources are available in-house, most organizations will naturally choose these options. External training will have its place, but possibly only for particular groups, such as apprentices or middle managers. If you are to be in a position to influence such decisions, you will need to be totally familiar with the cost and benefit implications of both internal and external training.

If training is to be provided externally, this does not mean that the trainer can simply pass on all responsibility to the provider. The training department will still be expected to

- advise on course suitability;
- book course places and accommodation and travel where needed;
- maintain close links with the relevant establishment;
- monitor trainees' progress;

- evaluate the training, see below;
- ensure that there is appropriate in-company debriefing and follow-up.

If the training is to be provided internally, sound planning and organizational skills and a detailed understanding of training methods, will be called for. The trainer's role is not necessarily that of instructor, and there will be many occasions when it will be more effective for line managers to provide the expert input on particular topics. For this reason, detailed knowledge of the subject matter is not always essential, although the trainer will need enough insight into it to be able to put together a logical programme and to advise on appropriate ways of approaching the material.

If you are to get involved in designing and running training courses, you will need training yourself. You will need to know how to tailor the methods and tutors you use to the needs of your trainees and their specific learning objectives. You will need to know when and how to use lectures, case studies, discussion groups, role plays, simulations, videos, business games and so forth.

You will need to be a skilled negotiator to persuade line managers and subject specialists to provide appropriate input. You will also need to be a subtle coach, briefing your tutors carefully and making sure the design and delivery of their sessions contributes to the achievement of the relevant objectives. And you will need to know when and how to evaluate the learning which has (or has not) taken place.

For many training specialists, it is only a short step from planning and organizing training courses to conducting some sessions themselves.

5. Presenting a Training Session

- Can you capture the attention of an audience, and retain it for more than a few minutes?
- Can you get inside what other people think and know about a subject, in order to put material across in terms *they* will understand?
- Can you always be sure that everyone present shares the same understanding of the messages you have been

trying to convey or the objectives you have been trying to achieve?

Very few people can do all these things instinctively. They call for a very subtle blend of timing, pace, insight and empathy. But the techniques involved can be learnt. On an appropriate presentational skills course, you will learn

- how to open and close a session,
- how to make and keep contact with your audience,
- how to involve them in your presentation,
- how to present material in a logical order,
- how to reinforce your message with well-chosen, carefully designed visual aids, and above all,
- how to achieve the objectives of your session.

You will need to work on the way your voice sounds to others – is it loud enough or too loud? Do you pronounce your words clearly enough? Do you tend to speak too quickly, or too slowly? Do you look at people while you are talking to them? Do you put your words together in a logical, grammatical order? Do you sound enthusiastic and sincere? And, since most presentations also involve writing things on flip-charts, white-boards or overhead projector transparencies, can you spell, and can you write clearly and neatly?

Very few training sessions are effective without some sort of audience involvement. If the session lasts more than twenty minutes, you will have exceeded most people's span of attention. If they do not actually fall asleep after this time, that does not mean they are still concentrating as effectively as they were at the start. So learning to involve your audience is a very important part of becoming an effective presenter. You can do this by asking questions. New trainers sometimes find it particularly difficult to phrase their questions in the right way. They do not want to make it too obvious what answer they are looking for – or the audience will feel they are playing guessing games. On the other hand, if the question is worded too indirectly or clumsily, the audience can't see what they are driving at. In those circumstances, trainees

can quickly become frustrated, feeling that they have failed in some way.

Putting trainees in groups, to get them 'working on an exercise', sometimes looks like an easier option. You may have encountered the kind of lecturer who makes this a regular feature – and nips off to the canteen for a cup of tea while the students do the work. In fact, designing or choosing group exercises, discussion topics and case studies, briefing the group, monitoring their progress to make sure their discussions will lead to the achievement of the relevant learning objectives, and debriefing them afterwards, are all skilled tasks. Helping the group to identify the correct learning points for themselves, takes a good deal more patience, interpersonal skill and knowledge of the subject than simply giving a presentation on the topic.

Whatever the preferred form of presenting training material at present in your organization, it is important to remember that learning is not just about soaking up information. It is about understanding and applying particular techniques or ways of working.

You can talk all day about how to operate a keyboard. You can get the group to discuss it or to answer questions about it. Afterwards, your audience may be able to tell anyone who is interested, all sorts of fascinating facts about what each of the keys will do. But ask them to type a letter and you may find they literally don't know where to start.

Similarly you can construct a very interesting and intellectually challenging course on the essentials of effective leadership, packed to bursting with exciting case studies and in-depth discussions. Yet you may turn out some of the best-informed most *ineffective* leaders your company has ever known.

This is because knowledge alone is not enough. It is only when your listeners have the chance to try it out for themselves, to 'get the feel of it', that learning really begins.

6. Evaluating Effectiveness

Evaluation is about trying to assess whether or not training has had the desired impact. This is one of the most intellectually challenging aspects of training. You may need to ask, or to help answer, a number of questions.

- Do the trainees feel as though they have benefited from their training? The simplest way to find out is to ask them – either face to face or via a questionnaire.
- Have the trainees learnt what they were intended to learn, that is, have the learning objectives been achieved? Some kind of test of the behaviour described in the learning objectives may need to be designed, administered, marked and the results recorded for future reference. This will be particularly important where training forms part of a National Vocational Qualification (NVQ) which requires the competence of trainees to be assessed and formally recorded in order to qualify for a nationally recognized certificate.

  Such *immediate* outcome evaluation will of course only indicate that trainees completing their training have acquired the necessary competence to perform. If they have not, this may indicate that the training was poorly designed or delivered – or that the trainees were not well-motivated.

It does not prove that they will apply this competence back in the job. The transfer of learning, from the training room to the realities of the working world, is often less than perfect – either because the training did not take full account of the circumstances in which trainees will be expected to perform, or because it did not reflect the actual working practices of the trainees' colleagues or bosses.

- Have the trainees applied what they have learnt, to bring about an improvement in the way they do their work? The answer to this can best come from a careful appraisal of performance. Managers can be asked to rate the competence level of trainees prior to training, and again afterwards. The mechanisms for doing this need to be designed, administered, recorded and analysed and due account will have to be taken of other factors which may have had an impact on the trainee's performance.

  Even if there appears to be a dramatic improvement in the performance of some individual trainees, this still does not prove that the training was worthwhile. For this, a further level of evaluation is needed.

- Is the organization as a whole achieving better results as a consequence of the training which has taken place? The answer to this question may demand considerable research. First of all, someone must decide what 'results' are relevant. Does your chief executive want to establish a link between the amount spent on training and the net profit of the company? Or would it be better to consider specific aspects of company performance – such as quantity of goods sold, number of rejects, number of customer complaints, level of staff turnover, and so forth?

  In theory, these *ultimate* outcomes of training should be the ones that really matter. In practice, the complexities and uncertainties involved deter many organizations from spending as much time on this aspect as they should. Some fall back on the belief that their sales would have been even lower, and their labour turnover even higher, if they hadn't done the training they did.

As you can see, the evaluation of training can be a major task, especially where a large number of training programmes – some internal and some external – are operating simultaneously. It is a vital part of the training process of which people new to the function are sometimes unaware. It calls for an objective, critical and analytical approach not always associated with the popular image of training. And yet it is absolutely crucial to the success of any training department. It is only by constantly reappraising the effectiveness of training that training programmes can be developed and redesigned to fulfil the needs of individuals and of the organization as a whole.

Who Does What?

The skills required to become an effective trainer take time to acquire. For this reason, some organizations employ training specialists who have little or no involvement with the rest of the work of the personnel department. The route into such roles may in fact be direct from line management, via an appropriate 'training to train' course, rather than from personnel.

A line management pedigree can give the trainer credibility with both trainees and their bosses. A period in training can also give line managers the opportunity to broaden and deepen their understanding of the business and its operational needs, and to develop their own coaching, counselling and interpersonal skills in a way which will be of value when they eventually return to a line management role.

Happily, the practice of 'shunting the dead wood' sideways into training – where it was perceived that they could wind down gracefully towards retirement – has now been discontinued by most major organizations. Instead, a period in the training team is now a key part of management development for future top managers.

Even though training may be seen as a specialist role within your organization's personnel department, it is, nevertheless, vital that the link between personnel and training is a close one. In particular:

- personnel specialists may need to provide input to management training programmes covering topics such as interview skills, handling disciplinary problems, equal opportunities, health and safety and other aspects of 'people management';

- trainers will need access to some items of personnel documentation. Performance appraisals (see Chapter Six), are just one example. The personnel team may be using appraisals to assess pay and promotion. The training team will want to know which areas of work could be improved by training and what specific training needs have been identified by job holders and their bosses;

- trainers will need to input some of the information which the personnel team require in order to assess skill levels and to assist in human resource planning. A common database, containing information about training received and planned, and the standards attained, will be of value to both departments;

- regular and effective communication between the two sections is vital. If the training team is responsible for ensuring that new recruits attend induction courses, they need to know who is starting work and when. If they are responsible for running pre-retirement courses, they will want to know who is due to retire. It is often on such points of administrative detail that the reputation of the personnel department as a whole is won or lost.

Whether or not there is a specialist team to provide training, line managers will have certain expectations of their personnel/training department. These will probably include:

- a carefully worked-out timetable of 'standard' courses – like induction, pre-retirement and core skills – programmed for at least the next twelve months, at times which suit the peaks and troughs in their own departmental workloads, at venues which are accessible to trainees and at a cost which they feel they can afford;

- professional advice on how to identify the training needs of their own staff, and appropriate mechanisms, such as performance appraisal, to help them do it;

- a quick response to new training needs which they identify, either for individuals or groups. They will also expect sensible decisions to be made about how, where and by whom such training can best be provided. They will expect the training plan to be sufficiently flexible to allow for some 'specials' and they will not usually expect an established training department to have to go outside for help unless this will clearly benefit the training by bringing in additional expertise or fresh insights;

- careful control of the training budget, to ensure that all expenditure is properly planned and that money is not wasted. With so many expensive aids on the market, from computer based training systems and interactive video to computer graphics packages and image scanners for the production of visual aids, the training team will often find themselves inundated with glossy brochures from manufacturers promising the last word in training technology. Line managers will expect the training specialists to assess each of these aids in terms of their potential value to the organization – and only to buy or rent when there is real benefit to be had, in terms of quality or quantity or cost savings in other areas. The acquisition of expensive white elephants, just to be at the forefront of technology or to keep the trainers amused between courses, is not something that most organizations will tolerate in their training departments;

- a streamlined and efficient administration system. Line managers will expect a simple but effective system of course nominations and confirmations, with joining instructions being sent to delegates in good time. They may expect the training department to handle accommodation and travel arrangements. They will certainly expect proper attendance and performance records to be kept and, possibly, a progress report on each of their people;

- professionally designed and presented in-house training programmes, using relevant, up-to-date material, geared to the needs of the business and drawing on the skills of internal and external subject 'experts' as appropriate;

- training sessions which are lively and interesting and which stretch those attending. They will not expect trainees to be able to treat training course as a holiday and they will expect the venues used, room-layout and housekeeping, equipment, visual aids, handouts and so forth, to be appropriate to the nature of the course;

- the right to contribute to the design and delivery of training courses for their own people. (Although some managers are content to hand their staff over to the training department without knowing exactly what will happen to them there, many more feel, quite rightly, that they should be involved;)

- careful evaluation of all training, both internal and external. They will not expect the training department to keep using colleges or consultancies which have failed to deliver an appropriate standard of training in the past. Nor will they expect to find that internal training course look the same now as they did five years ago. They will anticipate that proper evaluation will lead to continual refinements and that course development will be a key priority for trainers.

In some training teams, each trainer will take some responsibility for meeting all these expectations – in relation to perhaps just one area of training. So the person or group responsible for, say, clerical training, may handle all the nominations and administration as well as the design, presentation and evaluation aspects.

In others, the duties will be divided according to type. So one person or group may tackle administration, another design, a third presentation, and so on. Dealings with external training providers may all be channelled through one person/team or may be split according to the type of training or the employment category of those attending.

However it is organized, the training team can never work in isolation from line managers. They must work together to ensure

- new training needs are speedily and accurately identified;
- course material is relevant and up-to-date. Line managers need to be involved as directly as possible. They, after all, will be the losers if their people waste time acquiring obsolete skills or learning to do their jobs the wrong way;
- training is not just seen in terms of courses. Line managers have a major responsibility for the development of their people. In many instances, on-job coaching by their boss

will be a more effective and direct means of meeting an individual's training needs than attendance at an expensive off-job course. This means line managers themselves must be encouraged to acquire the skills necessary to help their people learn. They must be prepared to let people make mistakes and to help them think through alternative ways of doing things, without destroying self-confidence. This may not come easily to managers who may themselves be judged more on immediate results than on the long-term development of their people;

- appropriate follow-up is carried out. If there is to be any real chance that knowledge and skills acquired on training courses will be used to improve job performance, the trainee will need support when he or she returns to work. The manager or supervisor who says, 'You can forget all that rubbish they taught you at the training school, this is the way we do it here', must be made to see that this is quite simply an untenable state of affairs. Either the training at the school is inappropriate and must therefore be changed, or 'the way we do it here' is wrong – in terms of safety, quality, or some other consideration. If that is the case, it must be changed to conform to company standards;

- regular feedback is available to the training team. Unless trainers work with line management to find out how the training is perceived and to involve them in evaluation, training will be carried out in a vacuum. Sooner or later, the trainers will stop developing effective training, simply because they have been starved of the information they need to evaluate their success.

Who can Help?

If you need to look outside your organization to find suitable courses for employees, you will find that there is no shortage of training providers. Most are listed, together with details of the type of training which they offer, in the *National Training Index*.

Many business schools and consultancies also have extensive mailing lists and will send unsolicited details of forthcoming training events, so you can build up your own library of information. You will also find details of specific courses advertised in the relevant trade/professional journals. Some business and management courses are reviewed in the *Financial Times*.

Because there is such a wealth of information available, fighting your way through it can be a major problem. You will find that your local Pickup representative can help you here. His or her job is to establish links between employers and training establishments/colleges, to ensure that their needs are matched. You can find the address in the telephone directory.

Your local Training and Enterprise Council (TEC) should also be a useful source of information regarding training within your locality – and is charged with developing training activities to meet the needs of local employers. You should find their address, or that of the Training Agency which now works with the TEC, in the telephone directory.

Books

For a comprehensive introduction to the topic, consult

Training and Development, Rosemary Harrison, IPM 1988.

Training Interventions, Second edition, John Kenney and Margaret Reid, IPM 1989.

For more specialist aspects, have a look at

Everyone Needs a Mentor, Second edition, David Clutterbuck, IPM 1991.

Continuous Development: The path to improved performance, Ed Sue Wood, IPM 1988.

Evaluation: Relating training to business performance, Terence Jackson, Kogan Page, 1989.

Courses

If you are to develop your training activities in-house, your most immediate need may be for training for yourself. An IPM course, with specialist training modules at stage two, will be the most complete answer, but will take up to three years on a part-time basis, assuming you have the required entry qualifications (see Chapter Ten). Alternatively, a one-year Certificate in Personnel Practice course will usually place considerable emphasis on training skills.

Other shorter 'Training to Train' courses are also available. These include:

British Association for Commercial and Industrial Education (BACIE)
16 Park Crescent
London W1N 4AP
Tel: 071 635 5351;

Guardian Business Services
119 Farringdon Road
London EC1R 3DA
Tel: 071 278 6878;

Walpole Occupational Psychologists
61–63 St John Street
London EC1M 4AN
Tel: 071 253 2340;

British Institute of Management (BIM)
Management House
Cottingham Road
Corby
Northants NN17 1TT
Tel: 0536 204222

For details, consult the IPM Magazine *Personnel Management* or contact

Institute of Training and Development
Marlow House
Institute Road
Marlow
Bucks SL7 1BN
Tel: 0628 890123

For a full list of regular training activities run by the IPM, including courses, seminars and workshops, contact the Training Services Department.

Chapter Six

Performance Appraisal

Introduction

As we saw in Chapter Five, one of the best aids to identifying training needs and to evaluating the outcome of training is a systematic appraisal of performance. Such an appraisal has a number of other uses, too. These include:

- identifying barriers to effective performance. Lack of training may be one such barrier, but unclear objectives, ineffective job design, unwieldy systems, poor inter-personal relations, even the physical layout of the work-place, can all inhibit performance. Many of these things may go unremedied unless bosses and their subordinates sit down together from time to time to examine whether there are any ways in which matters can be improved. Performance appraisal interviews are an opportunity to do this:
- providing an objective basis for performance related pay (see Chapter Seven.) Many would argue that it is bad practice to discuss salaries during appraisal interviews – on the grounds that this tends to override other concerns. But if your organization is one where people are rewarded, at least partly, on the basis of the effort they put in or the results they achieve, some means of ensuring a well-balanced overview of these will be necessary. The performance appraisal system can at least provide a starting point;
- improving communications and developing a more partici-pative management style. In many organizations, people at different levels find it surprisingly hard to talk to each other. Information and ideas – about company objectives, problems and hopes for the future – which ought to be flowing back and forth regularly, don't. Although no

appraisal system will alter this over night, a carefully designed one, with committed and well-trained appraisers, can at least provide one forum for discussion;

- establishing some basic beliefs about what is important – in specific jobs and in the organization as a whole. For example, some chief executives are very concerned about health and safety, equal opportunities and other aspects of 'people care'. Yet they find that people lower down the business judge their own and their subordinates' performance solely by reference to sales results or output. By including reference to 'people care' issues at appraisal, it may be possible to start focusing attention on a broader range of what might be termed 'organizational values';
- letting employees know that their contribution is valued – and thereby motivating them to continue to give of their best. For example, the fact that your boss recognizes what you have achieved and is prepared to spend time talking through ways of helping you to achieve more, is likely to have a positive effect on your commitment and determination to succeed.

It will be for the personnel director/manager to explore, with his or her senior colleagues, the extent to which an appraisal system might be an appropriate way of tackling such issues in your organization.

What is Involved?

Most modern systems of appraisal have certain key characteristics.

- They are carried out at regular intervals – at least annually, and, particularly for new recruits, sometimes more frequently.
- Performance is appraised against specified criteria. Sometimes these relate specifically to the achievement of the key *results* which the job is designed to achieve. Sometimes more detailed descriptions of the sort of *behaviour* or *competences* associated with effective performance are used. Occasionally, lists of personality *traits* are still included.

- The job holder's performance is discussed, by the job holder (appraisee) and their boss (appraiser), at an interview. This is intended to give both parties an opportunity to explore how they see things, and, wherever possible, to agree a plan of action for the future.
- A written report is (usually) produced. Sometimes this is an unstructured narrative. More often, the criteria to be appraised are listed on a form, and performance is rated using some sort of alphabetical or numerical scale. Both appraiser and appraisee will usually be required to sign the report, and sometimes the appraiser's boss will countersign it. This is to help maintain consistency of assessment across different sections or departments.
- Follow-up action, such as further training, re-design of systems, or modifications to working practices, is taken by the appraiser and/or the appraisee. Sometimes other members of the organization, such as the appraiser's boss or the personnel department, will be called upon to assist.

There are a number of different steps involved in introducing and implementing an effective system.

1. Designing a Scheme

The task of actually designing an appraisal scheme is likely to fall to either a personnel or training specialist – or a combination of the two. But many organizations now recognize that divorcing the design of the scheme from the requirements of the users is a recipe, if not for disaster, then at least for lack of commitment from line managers. Appraisals are a very time-consuming part of many managers' jobs. Unless the scheme is designed to be highly relevant to their needs, many managers will simply not use it, or not use it properly. So whoever works out the 'nuts and bolts' of the scheme must liaise closely with line managers to make sure it is workable. If you are to be involved, you will need:

- a thorough understanding of the objectives of the scheme;
- a knowledge of alternative approaches – results, behaviour,

or traits-based criteria – and an understanding of how each would relate to the objectives which your scheme is designed to serve;
- the time, resources and skills required to analyse the appropriate appraisal criteria for each job or job-type in your organization;
- the interpersonal skills necessary to persuade senior managers to devote time and thought to identifying performance criteria and to consider issues such as the frequency and format of the appraisal;
- the communication skills necessary to write up the appropriate paperwork and associated user instructions and training briefs;
- the commonsense and understanding of business priorities to ensure you don't do anything silly – like setting up a scheme which demands large amounts of management time during peak trading periods.

2. Administering a Scheme

Some organizations operate an 'appraisal period' – that is a specified month or two months of the year in which all appraisals must be completed, countersigned and returned to the personnel or training department. Others operate a rolling appraisal cycle, perhaps linked to individual joining or appointment dates, or to birthdays.

Either way, someone must arrange for appropriate numbers of copies of the appraisal form to be printed and despatched to appraisers in good time for them to prepare for their appraisal interviews. In some schemes, the appraisee also has a form to complete, and these too must be sent out in good time.

Someone must keep a record of the date when the forms were despatched – and the dates on which they are returned. Someone must extract information from the completed forms to trigger specific action – whether that be a training course booking or a salary review.

And someone must collate the results of the appraisal, by job category, department, division or whatever unit is the most meaningful. This will help senior management to assess whether the scheme is being systematically and fairly applied across all parts of the business. If one department head is rating all his people as 'excellent' and another is rating all hers as 'below the required standard', some questions may need to be asked of both.

3. 'Policing' a Scheme

Any appraisal scheme is only as good as the people who use it. If the scheme does not fit their needs, or they cannot see how it will help them, people will not use it. Some personnel and training specialists find this frustrating. Having spent months designing a scheme, weeks training appraisers and appraisees in its use, and hours getting the forms printed and organizing the administration, it can be very galling to find that appraisal forms are not returned. Equally galling is the realization that some of the forms which *have* been returned bear all the hallmarks of having been written up by the appraiser in a moving railway carriage, miles from the appraisee. 'The whole purpose of the appraisal' you will cry in anguish, 'is that the appraiser and the appraisee should *agree* what goes on the form!'

In some personnel and training departments, the policing of the appraisal system becomes almost a full-time activity for someone at certain times of the year. They must cajole and persuade reluctant line managers at least to go through the motions of completing the form, so that the 'system' can be kept intact.

Perhaps some of this time could be more constructively spent trying to find out why people are so reluctant to use the system – and adapting it accordingly.

4. Appraisal Training

Systematic and objective appraisal of other people's performance does not come naturally to most of us. Subjective snap judgements, based on what the appraisee has said or done in the immediate past, are much easier for us to make. Because of this, and because of the need to make sure that appraisers have 'bought in' to the objectives of the scheme and understand the criteria upon which assessment is to be based, appraisal training is vital.

Some appraisal forms bear all the hallmarks of having been written in a moving railway carriage

The introduction, organization-wide, of a new or significantly revised appraisal system will create an organization-wide management training need. Over a short period of time, the training team will need to schedule enough courses to ensure that all who are to undertake appraisals receive appropriate training – in assessment against specified criteria, appraisal interviewing, the mechanics of the scheme and its administration – in so far as these affect line managers.

Because so many people will need to take part, the pressure will be on to keep the course as short as possible, without jeopardizing its effectiveness. It will also need to be designed to achieve the same objectives with people at very different levels in the organization's hierarchy. If the scheme is to have real credibility, the board of directors must be as well versed as the most junior supervisor – because both must be seen to use it effectively. (This is not to suggest that appraisal criteria will be the same from senior management to shop floor –

only that the general principles of appraisal may be common to both.)

As a follow-up to the training course itself, it may also be necessary to set up an appraisal 'help-line' for a while. Appropriately trained personnel staff can deal with telephone queries from appraisers or appraisees who are uncertain about particular aspects of the scheme.

5. Follow-up

In addition to the types of regular follow-up already described, the personnel department can use the information provided via the appraisal system to develop a number of individual and group follow-up activities. These will range from planning career moves for particular individuals through to the development of new training programmes to meet common training needs.

Indeed, the careful analysis of the trends emerging from appraisal will be one of the main inputs to the drawing up of the training plan for the following year. There is little point in scheduling fifteen interview skills training courses in the next twelve months if the appraisal forms suggest that most are now reasonably competent in this area. Instead, the focus may need to change, to financial awareness or computer literacy – or whatever the appraisals suggest is the most serious gap in the skills base.

Who Does What?

Appraisal is a tool which assists in the overall development of human resources, rather than being a personnel department tool as such. Appraisal systems should, therefore, be designed with line managers for use by line managers.

Line managers will expect the personnel specialist to:

- advise on the objectives of the scheme;
- suggest alternative approaches;
- assist in the identification of appropriate criteria;
- advise on the appropriate format for the written report;
- develop and implement appropriate training;

- supply the paperwork and an appropriate timetable for completion;
- carry out the necessary administration;
- analyse appraisal reports and take follow-up action;
- evaluate the effectiveness of the scheme and suggest modifications or redesign as appropriate.

Where it is not practicable to involve all line managers at every stage in the design and development of a scheme, it may be necessary to set up a joint personnel/line management working party, drawn from the appropriate parts of the business. This will ensure that line managers are involved in

- determining whether or not performance appraisal is relevant to the needs of the organization;
- specifying the particular objectives which they would like the scheme to meet;
- identifying the criteria which best distinguish between effective and ineffective performance in the jobs in their departments;
- commenting on the feasibility of alternative formats and schedules.

Once the scheme has been introduced, all line managers will be involved in

- careful planning before they interview each of their subordinates to make sure that the discussion focuses on achievements as well as development points;
- conducting *constructive* appraisal interviews, designed to achieve the objectives of the scheme. This should mean that appraisees leave the interview with a clear understanding of how they are performing in relation to the requirements of their job, with positive ideas on what they can do to develop themselves and their performance further, and with the motivation and commitment to strive to achieve it;
- making sure that follow-up action is initiated and monitored. Any commitments made during the interview must be honoured. Agreed changes in working practices should be installed and monitored. On-job coaching should

begin at the very first opportunity. The personnel/training department must be chased up if they don't come forward with a date for necessary training, and so forth;
- using the appraisal discussion and report as the basis for a continuing dialogue throughout the period between appraisals;
- providing feedback to the personnel department regarding the working of the scheme and, where necessary, making suggestions for revising or developing it.

Who Can Help?

Many management consultants will help you to design a new appraisal system or to overhaul an old one. They can be particularly helpful in managing the kind of in-depth study of effective versus ineffective behaviour which will be needed to establish relevant and soundly-based appraisal criteria. They will also generally be prepared to help train appraisers and appraisees in the use of the scheme, and will often produce the first run of forms, booklets, and other documentation for you.

If you feel you have, or could develop, the necessary expertise in-house, there are several other sources of assistance.

Books

For a general overview of appraisal, consult

> *Staff Appraisal: The first step to effective leadership*, Gerry Randell, Peter Packard and John Slater, IPM 1984.

or

> *Practical Performance Appraisal*, Valerie and Andrew Stewart, Gower, 1978.

For an analysis of current practice, and examples of other companies' documentation (which may help you to develop your ideas but is *not* likely to transfer happily to your organization unless circumstances are identical) refer to

Performance Appraisal Revisited, Phil Long, IPM 1986.

For more general advice on appraisal, try

Success in Management: Personnel, Third edition, Penny Hackett, John Murray, 1990.
or
Performance Appraisal and Career Development, Clive Fletcher and Richard Williams, Hutchinson, 1985.

Courses

A number of reputable bodies offer short courses on the design of appraisal systems and/or appraisal interview skills. For details, contact the IPM, Croner Conferences, or the Industrial Society.

Chapter Seven

Rewards

Introduction

Few things excite more debate and suspicion than the revision of the company car policy or the introduction of a new bonus scheme. Sound and effective reward strategies seldom arouse comment. Unfair or ineptly managed ones can do real damage to recruitment, retention and productivity.

The design and implementation of an organization's remuneration policy is, therefore, one of the most contentious aspects of the work of the personnel department. It can also be one of the most complex. The rewards which employees will expect for their work are many and various. Most people will expect:

1. A rate of *basic pay* which is
- fair when compared with that paid elsewhere for the same type of work – that is, appropriate relative pay;
- fair when compared with that paid to others doing the same type of work within the organization, and in relation to others doing more or less demanding work – that is, an appropriate pay structure and pay differentials;
- fair in relation to the employee's own investment, in terms of effort expended, or results achieved, or time served, or qualifications obtained, or a combination of two or more of these – that is, an appropriate pay system;

2. Some additional reward or recognition for service above and beyond the call of duty, such as working unsocial hours, shifts or overtime – that is, appropriate *premium payments*;

3. A set of *terms and conditions* of employment which allow for reasonable hours of work, rest periods, holidays, sick pay and pensions comparable with those available in the rest of the industry.

Some will also expect a range of additional *benefits* – from private medical insurance and an executive pension to a company car and access to the directors' dining room.

In many organizations, rewards differ for different groups of employees. So you might find that directors have one sort of 'package', senior staff have another, junior staff another, and shop floor workers may have packages which differ according to which trade union, and hence which negotiating group, they belong to. The more fragmented things are, the harder it will be to avoid the divisions and hostility which arise when one group believes another is getting better treatment.

Because of the difficulties inherent in such fragmentation, some more enlightened companies adopt a policy of *harmonization*. In its most complete form, this means just one pay structure and one set of terms, conditions and benefits, from top to bottom of the organization. Everyone is paid a monthly salary rather than an hourly or weekly wage. Everyone has the same hours of work, sick pay and redundancy arrangements, pension scheme and holiday entitlement, and everyone eats in the same canteen.

What is Involved?

It will be for the personnel director and board colleagues to decide the overall approach to pay and conditions in your organization. It will be they, rather than more junior members of the personnel team, who set the organization's pay policy. Because this policy will influence all aspects of your work if you become involved in designing or administering rewards, we will start by examining some of the things which may have influenced your board in formulating their policy.

Beliefs about collectivism versus individualism. Because differences in rewards can be divisive, it sometimes seems simpler to aim for a reward policy which treats people collectively, as part of a group, and plays down the individual differences in the way they do their work or the results they achieve. Where collectivism prevails, any differences in rewards are likely to be related to non contentious things like length of service. After all, if all one has to do to get a pay rise is to put in another year's service, everyone can see that they are basically on an equal footing.

In such organizations, relatively impersonal and bureaucratic systems, which place emphasis on the jobs rather than the people, are likely to be used to determine pay. So *job evaluation* may be used to determine the relative size of each of the jobs in the organization. Jobs are then graded, and promotion from one grade to another may be controlled by a committee or promotions board. Within each grade, pay is based on length of service.

Such an approach tends to suit large, stable organizations, where the pace of change is slow and there are many people all doing the same or very similar work, according to prescribed systems, with little scope for personal initiative. But in more dynamic, fast-changing companies, where the skills and energy of key individuals can really make the difference between success and failure for the enterprise, it would tend to stifle innovation.

In such a situation, many would argue for a more individualistic approach, rewarding each person for what they contribute. The market rate which the individual could command elsewhere, and/or bonuses and performance payments related to the benefits he or she is perceived to have brought to the organization, may provide a suitably flexible framework. The person, rather than the job, will be the focus.

If this more individualistic approach is to benefit the organization in the longer term, it must be seen to be fair. Objective and consistent criteria must be used when assessing each individual's contribution. If employees cannot see what it takes to reach the highest level of rewards, they may become demotivated. This may be reflected in high labour turnover and disputed rates, and low productivity.

If too much subjectivity creeps into decisions about pay, there is also a danger of unfair discrimination – between men and women or between ethnic groups. (The Equal Pay Act, 1970 and the Equal Value Regulations, 1983 seek to prevent sex-based differences in pay. The more subjective a pay system becomes, the harder it may be to establish that differences in pay between men and women doing work which appears to outsiders to be of equivalent value, are in fact based on something other than sex.)

Beliefs about motivation. The part that financial rewards play in encouraging people to work, or to work harder, has long been a subject for research and debate. There are those who believe that people work only for money and that direct financial incentives are the best way of attracting and retaining them and of maximizing their productivity. Those who hold this view will tend to design pay systems which link pay to performance as directly as possible, choosing to pay by results.

Others take the view that people can be motivated by the satisfaction to be gained from the work itself. Provided their pay is adequate to their needs, they will not work harder to increase it. If, however, their pay falls below a minimum acceptable level, they will become demotivated. Those who hold this view will tend to opt for systems which allow for competitive basic rates of pay, without additional bonuses or incentive schemes.

Yet a third view is that people differ in the degree of importance which they attach to financial rewards and in the way they think about their pay. We don't all share the same values, this group would argue. And unless we can see that by working hard we will achieve something we *do* value – be it a better car, promotion, or the respect of our colleagues – we won't pull out all the stops. Pay policies derived from this point of view tend to be more flexible, perhaps even building in elements of what is known as the 'cafeteria approach'. This means that individual employees have some scope to choose how their reward package is made up.

The perceived importance of 'inputs' (effort) versus 'outputs' (results). If rewards *are* to be designed to motivate people, it is important to decide what they are to be rewarded *for*. Where specific results are hard to measure or to attribute to particular individuals, it may not be easy to reward 'outputs'. On the other hand, to reward only 'inputs' such as effort, experience, qualifications, may mean rewarding people highly for achieving very little. This can be expensive.

The need to control costs. The smaller the margin between the price an organization can get for selling its goods or services and the cost of making or providing them, and the larger the payroll as a proportion of those costs, the more emphasis there is likely to be on controlling costs. The more directly payment to employees can be linked to output produced, the easier this will be.

Where cost control is of paramount importance, you may find extensive use of payment by results systems which reduce the chance that people will have to be paid merely for 'turning up'. Short term contracts, or the use of agency staff in place of permanent employees, may also be favoured as a way of minimizing the overhead cost of labour. The personnel practitioner who wishes to suggest a move away from such practices may encounter resistance on the grounds that costs will rise.

Trade union power. Management does not always have a free hand to design the ideal reward package. The trade unions with whom they negotiate may have strong views on how big the package should be, and on how it should be made up. Sometimes any attempt to formulate a coherent new pay policy is submerged by the apparently more pressing need to buy off union hostility or avoid strike action.

If you are operating in a unionized environment, you will certainly find that union values and attitudes, as well as those of management, are a major influence on the way things are done. For example, traditional trade unions may be reluctant to accept performance related pay unless this is based only on quantifiable output. More generalized 'merit' payments may be mistrusted on the grounds that they encourage individualism rather than collectivism.

The need to compete in the labour market. Whatever other factors influence your organization's pay policy, your reward package must be attractive enough to persuade people of the right calibre to join and stay with you. Pay levels, and the composition of the package offered by other local (or in some cases national or international) employers competing for the same types of employee, are therefore bound to have a bearing. Some companies are particularly keen to obtain the prestige which is seen to come from being a 'market leader' in pay terms. Others are content with a more middle of the road position.

Reconciling all these different influences and values is not easy. In some organizations, they may never have been explicitly thought through and discussed. As a result, there may be no really clear statement of policy with regard to rewarding employees. So the design and implementation of pay systems and structures may owe more to *ad hoc* responses to particular situations than to the pursuit of a coherent philosophy.

If you are to be involved in dealing with rewards, you should first try to establish whether your organization does have a formal policy on pay. If it does not, it may be advisable to have a serious discussion with your boss, to clarify matters.

Within the framework provided by your organization's policy, there is a very wide range of reward–related activities in which you are likely to be involved. These are summarized below:

1. Job Evaluation

If your pay policy is based on the belief that the size of a job should influence the rewards of the job holder, the chances are that some form of job evaluation will be in operation.

There are many different job evaluation schemes, but all are designed to establish the relative worth of a number of different jobs. They do this by reference to the content of the jobs themselves, and/or to the demands which they make on the job holder in terms of knowledge, physical or mental effort, and other factors. Depending upon the level at which you are operating within the personnel team, you may be asked:

- to advise on the choice of scheme. Many reputable firms of management consultants have their own tried and tested schemes. Although this can be expensive, the consequences of trying to introduce an ill-thought-out scheme can be so costly it will often be worth investing in one which
  - is flexible enough to cover the range of jobs under review;
  - is reasonably simple to operate;
  - will be accompanied by appropriate briefing information and by training for evaluators and administrators;
  - does not include any sex-based criteria;
  - has a good track record for establishing grading structures which are felt to be fair, in organizations of similar size and complexity to your own;
  - can (ideally) be linked to up-to-date information about reward levels in other user organizations;
- to prepare or collate standardized, accurate and up-to-date job descriptions – using the format required for your particular scheme;
- to become a member of a job evaluation panel or committee. This in turn will involve being trained to look at each job description systematically and objectively, using the criteria laid down by your scheme;
- to administer the scheme, making sure that panels of trained evaluators are convened at regular intervals, that all jobs eligible for evaluation are considered by the panel, and that job holders and their bosses are advised of the results of the evaluation and of any consequent changes in grade or pay. In a large organization where the redesign of jobs or the creation of new ones is a regular occurrence, this can become almost a full-time job;
- to brief and/or train other people in the use of the

scheme, and to deal with enquiries from line managers and employees. Since job evaluation schemes are not universally popular, especially with those who believe their own job to have been under-graded, queries and comments will need careful handling. No scheme is perfect – but most are a good deal better than nothing. You will need to be able to handle doubters positively and constructively, without bringing your scheme into disrepute;
- to monitor the impact of the scheme, in terms of cost and employee reactions.

2. Assessing Market Rates

If your pay policy is to reward people competitively, you will need information about what your competitors are offering. Depending on your particular role, you may be asked:

- to analyse published pay surveys – perhaps provided by the consultants who are assisting with your job evaluation, perhaps from independent sources. You will need enough grasp of the statistical terms used in such surveys to enable you to make sense of the data;
- to design and/or conduct your own pay survey. This could involve analysis of job advertisements and discussion with 'experts' such as the local Jobcentre manager. Or it might mean identifying a group of companies with whom you are competing for staff and compiling a structured interview checklist or questionnaire as a means of obtaining comparative information.

   If you are to retain the co-operation of your sample of employers, you will need to approach them as professionally as possible, to obtain factual information about their current practice with regard to pay levels, overtime and other premia, bonuses and other terms and conditions of employment. You will need the statistical skills to analyse the data you collect, and report writing and/or presentation skills to communicate your findings;
- to assess the rewards assigned to particular jobs in relation to those elsewhere – and make recommendations for change. Here too, your report writing and presentation

skills could make a difference to the way management regard your proposals.

3. Grading Structures

Very few organizations pay all their employees the same amount. Most have some sort of hierarchy of pay, whether or not this is based on job evaluation. If it is based on job evaluation, jobs which are evaluated as being of similar value will be grouped together in one grade, with bigger jobs above them and those of lesser value below them. This provides a basic grade structure.

If your pay policy indicates that individuals should be rewarded on the basis not only of the size of their job but also according to individual criteria – be they effort, result or length of service related – you will need a band or ranges of pay for each grade.

A number of different salary points may be indicated within the grade and individuals will be placed on the appropriate salary using the relevant individual criteria. Alternatively, only the top and bottom salary levels for the grade may be quoted, and people will be slotted in at any point between the two, again on the basis of the specified criteria.

You may be involved in:

● designing and/or costing out possible structures. You will need a clear understanding of the mathematical principles involved in designing a pay structure, and must not lose sight of the objectives your own organization wishes to meet. Some of the questions which will require consideration include:
  – should one grade overlap with another so that novices in the higher grade are paid less than old hands in the lower grade?
  – should pay differentials between grades get bigger or smaller towards the top end of the hierarchy?
  – should the percentage difference between the top and bottom of a grade remain constant all the way up the structure?

These are just some of the important issues to be addressed.

Far from being just a paper exercise, the mathematical conclusions you reach when designing such a structure can make a big difference to whether people will strive to climb the ladder through promotion, or sit patiently at the bottom waiting for their next annual increment;

- communicating with other people about the structure and how it works. The specific tasks involved range from typing the pay scale and accompanying 'rules', to holding briefing meetings with line managers and employees or answering individual queries. What do people have to do to move up within their grade? Is there a specific link with performance appraisal? If so, how does it work? What do people have to do to get from one grade to another? Can they have their jobs re-evaluated on request, or is there a time limit between evaluations?

  Because many people will set a lot of store by the answers to questions such as these, your response can be crucial to the way in which other employees feel they are being treated. If you lead an employee, or his or her boss, to expect that there is more money on the way, woe betide you if it doesn't materialize;
- administering the system. Once the grading structure is in place, and the answers to questions such as those posed above have been decided, you or your personnel colleagues may be charged with making sure that the machinery operates smoothly.

  So if all those who are awarded top ratings at performance appraisal are entitled to a 12 per cent increase in pay, it may be your job to put that through, on the personnel information system and to the payroll department – not forgetting to follow that up with individual notifications to those concerned. Or if movement through grade is based on length of service, you may be the person who sends a note to managers or supervisors a few weeks before the due date, to confirm that the increase is to be actioned.

  Sometimes administration is routine and closely prescribed, with each person entitled to a one-step increment, once per year, no more and no less. There is no decision to be made, because the rules of the scheme have been clearly set out, and no deviation is permitted.

Sometimes an element of judgement or interpretation remains, where, for example, a scheme allows for larger or smaller increases on management recommendation. The managers must be asked to consider carefully the implications of any proposed adjustments, to make sure they are not establishing a precedent, for themselves or others, which could prove problematic in future.

Whichever approach is adopted, meticulous recording of all changes in pay, with dates and reasons, is essential;

- monitoring effectiveness. Particularly following the introduction of new pay structures, the board will expect some formal assessment of how much the changes have cost, and how they are working.

4. Collective Bargaining

If your organization recognizes one or more independent trade unions as representing the interests of some or all of its employees, pay negotiations, usually on an annual cycle, will be a regular feature. Here too there are a range of different activities in which personnel specialists are likely to get involved, including:

- collecting information about the 'going rate' among other companies (see above);
- helping to prepare management's negotiating position. However strong is their desire to control costs, and however small the amount they are prepared to put 'on the table', there will always be several different ways of approaching negotiations. Should we go for a larger percentage increase now, and no more for eighteen months? What about putting less on basic pay and more on bonus and/or pension and/or sick pay? What are the implications of giving something extra to those at the top of the scale, and not so much to those at the bottom – or vice versa? How realistic is it to hope that a 12 per cent increase in pay will be 'paid for' by a 14 per cent increase in productivity? Would it be safer to go for a 10 per cent increase in both?

The 'what if' questions are endless, and management cannot afford to go into negotiations without answers to most of them already worked out. (This is where the sort of computer modelling facility described in Chapter Two could really come into its own. Without it, you and your calculator will be working overtime.)

- taking part in negotiations. However well you feel you know the trade union representatives with whom you will be required to deal, you will find that formal negotiations require skilful handling. It is not just a question of guessing what the other side will demand and trying to pre-empt their position. The process is rather more subtle than that. To be effective, you will need specialist training. This can come either from carefully structured observation of in-house negotiations followed by debriefing by a skilled negotiator, or from attendance at an external negotiating skills course, or a combination of the two;
- minuting negotiations. In view of the number of offers and revised offers which are sometimes issued during a tough negotiating round, keeping track of *exactly* what the terms of the final agreement were, is vital. Whatever the virtues of the final settlement, they will certainly be forfeit if there is subsequent confusion over what was agreed. So even if you never say a word while the negotiations are in progress, your secretarial competence could make an important difference to the ultimate outcome!

5. Annual Reviews (cost of living increases)

Whether or not there is a regular negotiating cycle, most employees expect their pay to keep pace with inflation, and/or with increases paid to comparable employees elsewhere. Whether or not there are increments or merit payments due to individuals, if the anniversary of the last adjustment to their basic pay passes without some indication that a review is in hand, they will want to know why.

If you are unionized, this review date will be agreed with the union(s). If your rates of pay are influenced by a Wages Council, you will need to implement any changes from the date appointed by them. In other cases, the review date may be written into the employee's contract of employment.

Whenever the review date is, the implementation of a 'general award' as the cost of living increase is sometimes called, can be a major task for all in the personnel department – particularly if line managers have any discretion over whether or not everyone is entitled to the award. Quite apart from calculating the revised rates of pay, and notifying every line manager of existing and proposed revised rates, responses must be closely checked to make sure that people don't miss out simply because their boss has been slow in replying.

Even where the cost of living increase is automatic, the updating of individual records and communication with the payroll department can again mean that you and your colleagues will be working overtime.

6. Rewarding Performance

As well as, or instead of, a graded pay structure with scope for promotion between grades, your pay policy may call for some further ways of recognizing the performance of individuals or groups of employees. This could take the form of a payment by results system, commission, or an individual or group bonus.

Because such payments are linked directly to output or results, in some organizations it is line management who design and administer these additional types of reward. But in any company where the personnel department is charged with ensuring that pay policy is being implemented fairly and cost effectively, it is important that its members keep a 'watching brief' over their development.

You may be asked to help by:

- reviewing current practice – elsewhere in the industry and/or among your competitors. Published sources, such as those available from Incomes Data Services will help you here, as can your trade or professional association, if you belong to one;
- designing and/or costing out possible schemes. You will need a clear idea of the performance to be rewarded, and the proportion of basic pay which the additional payment should comprise. You will need to analyse past performance, to see what people can realistically be expected to achieve, and, in consultation with your

line management colleagues, decide where to pitch the target.

A word of warning is called for here. Designing incentive schemes and bonus systems often looks simple. Many an enthusiastic line manager will tell you: 'If we just give them an extra fiver every time they beat last week's figure, we'll hit our sales target in no time.' But has he or she really asked:

- is a 'fiver' enough to spur the group to maximum effort?
- is just 'beating' the previous week's figure enough to ensure hitting the sales target? If trade is at all seasonal, there may be some periods when a considerable increase is needed to achieve the overall plan;
- is paying an extra 'fiver' per week to everyone going to cost more than the extra revenue generated? Only if the new payment will represent the same percentage of sales, (or less) as basic pay, is the exercise likely to be really worthwhile;
- will staff be so greedy for the extra money that they will only think in the short term? Many sales organizations are now trying to build a reputation for customer care. Pushy sales people, desperate for a 'quick kill', can undo months of expensive customer care training. If you want customer care as well as sales, your incentive scheme should be designed to reward both;

- briefing people on the scheme and how it works. The whole point of any incentive scheme is that people should be motivated to earn the extra rewards on offer. Especially when new schemes are introduced, it is important that everyone understands clearly what they have to do to qualify for payment. The preparation of briefing notes, presentations on the scheme and how it works, and responses to individual queries from potential recipients and their bosses, may all fall to the staff of the personnel department;
- administering the scheme. It will usually be for line management to confirm that targets have been met and that any other relevant criteria have been satisfied. But personnel may be expected to do a certain amount of 'policing' – for example, carrying out spot checks against sales or production records to verify that the

necessary calculations have been carried out correctly –
before recording the amounts and passing them through
to payroll;
- monitoring the effectiveness of the scheme. Someone must
work out whether 'a fiver for beating last week's figures'
is proving cost-effective. The board will almost certainly
expect periodic reports on any scheme which affects a
significant number of employees or constitutes a sizeable
portion of payroll costs.

7. Premium Payments

Some of your employees may have to work unsocial hours.
Others may get particularly dirty in the course of their work,
or encounter particular hazards. If they do, they will expect,
and your reward policy should allow for, some compensation
for this. You may be involved in:

- researching current practice in other companies;
- designing and/or costing out alternative approaches,
bearing in mind the implications for differentials and
the impact on total remuneration. It may be more cost-
effective in the longer term, and may give more positive
signals to your workforce, to opt for what is known as
a 'clean' salary. Instead of lots of small allowances which
are costly to administer and open to abuse, everyone is
paid an enhanced basic rate – on the understanding that
when extra work or difficult conditions are encountered,
the compensation is already built into their earnings;
- briefing people on their entitlements. As a bank holiday
approaches, you can always expect a rush of queries along
the lines, 'I need a couple of my people in on Easter
Monday. Do they get double time, or a day off in lieu
– or both?'
- administering the payments and notifying payroll of which
employees are entitled to what. If the amount of a particular
allowance is subject to periodic review, you may also need
to make sure that these are actioned at the right time, and
that employees are kept informed of any changes;
- monitoring costs. Your board may want to keep a close
eye on, for example, the amount of overtime being worked

in particular departments or overall. A monthly report, highlighting this can help to identify high cost areas.

8. Terms and Conditions of Employment

Whether there is one set of terms and conditions in your organization, or twenty, someone must make sure that:

(i)   they all comply with minimum legal requirements;

(ii) they are pitched at an appropriate level in comparison with those elsewhere;

(iii) they are compatible with the organization's pay policy;

(iv) employees and their bosses know what they are;

(v) they are administered fairly and efficiently;

(vi) their costs are monitored and, wherever feasible, cost savings are introduced.

The range of items to be dealt with under this heading will include anything which properly forms part of the contract of employment. For example:

- hours of work   – days of the week
  - – start time
  - – finish time
  - – lunch/tea breaks, paid or unpaid
- holidays   – timing
  - – amount
  - – payment arrangements
- rate of pay and method of calculation
- pay interval   – hourly/weekly/monthly
- overtime   – notice and payment
- pay method   – cash/cheque/bank transfer
- sick pay   – procedure for notification of absence
  - – entitlement to Statutory Sick Pay
  - – entitlement to company sick pay
  - – timing/method of payment
- pensions   – membership of the State Earnings Related Pension Scheme

	– occupational pension scheme details
• maternity/ paternity leave	– procedure for notification of absence and return
	– entitlement to Statutory Maternity Pay
	– entitlement to company maternity pay
	– timing/method of payment
• other time off (compassionate leave, training leave, public duties, trade union duties)	– circumstances in which leave will be granted
	– notification arrangements
	– eligibility for payment
• other specific benefits (uniform, company car)	– basis of allocation
	– employee responsibilities
• grievance/disputes and disciplinary arrangements	– procedures and employee rights and obligations.
• notice	– requirements and payment

(We have already considered basic and premium payments and will discuss grievance and disciplinary procedures in later chapters.)

Deciding how best to approach all these issues is not a job for a novice. Because each of these items forms part of a legally enforceable contract, it is important to make sure that each is carefully thought through. Some require specific legal knowledge – such as the rules which apply to occupational pension schemes and their relationship with the state scheme. The procedures to be followed in dealing with Statutory Sick Pay or Statutory Maternity Pay provide other examples.

Your work in the personnel department may demand that you become expert in one or more of these areas. You may, for instance, need to learn exactly what constitutes a Period of Incapacity for Work, a Qualifying Day and a Period of Entitlement to sick pay – and to be able to explain them to line managers and employees who regard all this as just so much bureaucratic red tape. Or you may need to become familiar with the paperwork associated with maternity leave and maternity benefits, diarizing expected dates of return and sending out letters of enquiry to establish whether the employee plans to return to work.

Even something as apparently simple as holiday entitlements can mean that you need to get to grips with the answers to quite a wide range of questions. For example:

- how is entitlement calculated in the first year of service?
- what happens if someone leaves part way through the year, having taken more (or less) holiday than they are entitled to?
- what happens if they don't take all their holiday during the holiday year – can they carry it over till next year?
- does the holiday year start on 1 January – or some other date?
- who has the authority to agree holiday dates?
- whose job is it to keep track of how much holiday each employee has taken?
- what happens if someone is taken ill while on holiday?

In some organizations, the administration of the company car scheme also falls to the lot of the personnel department. If you are responsible for this you may need to be prepared for a lot of heated debate. Any revision to the policy, however well-intentioned, will stir up a hornets nest of people who had all but chosen the upholstery fabric of their new model, only to find they are now eligible for something different. Even where the policy allows for a cafeteria approach, enabling employees to pay extra for a car of their choice, arguments over the basic level of entitlement can still cause problems.

If you are to handle the purchase or leasing arrangements with external sources, your negotiating skills, as well as your familiarity with the subtle nuances of manufacturers' specifications, will be in demand.

If some of your employees are issued with a company

uniform, you may find that you are called upon to be a dress designer as well as a negotiator and administrator! Although line management will naturally want to be closely involved in any changes in uniform design, it is sometimes the staff dress administrator in the personnel department who has to come up with the initial proposals – and liaise with manufacturers over materials, delivery dates and so on.

Like cars, uniforms are often close to the hearts of recipients, and it is not always possible to please all the people all the time. One way of minimizing the negative effects of this is to run a uniform competition when your current staff dress is in need of an update. Any essential criteria, such as compatibility with the corporate colour scheme, ease of washing and wearing, cost and so forth, can be specified and a panel of judges appointed. For the personnel administrator whose fashion sense is less than perfect, this can be a real help.

Progress chasing consignments of uniform or arguing the toss on delivery dates with a car salesman may not be your idea of what personnel work is all about. But however innovative and proactive your personnel department is in other respects, one major 'foul up' on cars or uniforms can do severe damage to its reputation.

(The same could be said of canteens and recreational facilities for staff. Because these do not usually feature in the contract of employment, we will consider them in Chapter Nine under the heading of employee services, rather than as conditions of employment.)

Who Does What?

In all but the smallest organizations, personnel and payroll are likely to be separate departments. It is important that each understands the limits of its authority. In pay matters, it will usually be the personnel department which works with line management to clarify objectives and design the appropriate payment systems.

Liaison with the payroll department is, however, very important, even at the design stage. Many is the incentive scheme which has totally failed to achieve its objectives, simply because it was too complex for the payroll system to handle. However good such schemes may sound, they will serve little purpose until employees can see the extra money in their hands or on their pay slip. If the money turns up two months late, or not at all, they will soon lose interest.

Once appropriate pay structures and systems have been installed, it will be for personnel to keep payroll informed of changes in each employee's weekly or monthly entitlement. Payroll will calculate the amount to be deducted for income tax and national insurance and pension, make up the pay packets or arrange payment through bank transfer or Giro, and issue an itemized pay statement to each employee.

In addition, line management will expect personnel to:

- keep up to date with developments in the level and type of rewards offered elsewhere;
- monitor and advise on adjustments in the organization's own packages and structures;
- publish guidelines for line managers to help them to ensure that the decisions which they take regarding their own people are in line with agreed company policy and approved practice;
- advise line management on the interpretation of policies and procedures, with as much flexibility as possible – see below;
- do everything practicable to reduce the chances of line management getting involved in unproductive and costly arguments over pay – by handling union negotiations professionally and ensuring that rules are implemented evenhandedly;
- operate a smooth and efficient administration system so that all employees are informed of, and receive, the rewards to which they are entitled;
- liaise with payroll to ensure that any changes are actioned promptly. This is particularly important in the case of new joiners, who will generally expect to be paid on the first pay day after they start work. It is also crucial in the case of leavers. Most cost-conscious line managers do not take kindly to seeing the wages of an ex-employee as an item on their departmental expenditure statement;

- keep accurate and up-to-date records of everything from individual rates of pay, car allowances and holiday entitlements, to minutes of job evaluation committee meetings and trade union pay negotiations.

In return, line managers will usually:

- have ideas on the design of appropriate reward packages for particular groups of employees;
- take part (after training) in job evaluation committees and negotiating teams, where appropriate;
- supply accurate information about the work employees are doing and the standards they are achieving – for job evaluation and merit pay;
- exercise appropriate discretion over pay matters. Even if the chief designer does think that the pay the design team get is lousy, he or she will accomplish little by telling them so. It would be far better to concentrate on convincing the personnel director and the board;

Exercise appropriate discretion over pay matters

- manage their remuneration budgets sensibly. Just because the factory manager has a bit left in this year's budget, he or she does not need to set a precedent for next year by paying it out in extra bonuses.

The extent to which line managers will themselves wish to be involved in decisions affecting the pay of individual employees will depend upon the style and culture of the organization and the degree of variability allowed in pay. In a strongly centralized organization, where few decisions are devolved to line managers, individual's pay may be fixed by personnel in accordance with the rules of the job evaluation and grading schemes. In a decentralized climate, where each line manager is held directly responsible for the results achieved through his or her people, they will usually be less ready to let 'the system' dictate how people are rewarded.

Who Can Help?

If you are thinking of introducing job evaluation, radically revising a pay structure or introducing a major new bonus scheme, you would be well-advised to seek specialist help from a consultant, at least in the early stages. The more reputable firms will be happy to train your own staff to implement their system, and will 'bow out' once you are self sufficient in its use.

Any particular concerns you may have about equal pay for work of equal value could be discussed with the Equal Opportunities Commission. These and other pay matters can also be explored with the Advisory Conciliation and Arbitration Service (ACAS).

It is, however, easy to overlook the resources on your own door step. The importance of line management involvement in the development of workable reward strategies cannot be over-stressed. The workforce, too, can help. Many companies now undertake periodic attitude surveys among employees. One spin-off from this can be a much more soundly-based understanding of the sort of rewards which your employees would really value.

Nor is there any shortage of published material. In addition to the books listed below, Incomes Data Services issue periodic Reports, Briefs and Studies which will help you to keep up to date with movements in pay levels, changes in the composition of the reward packages offered by other employers, legal developments and general trends in pay.

Books

For a general overview of the design and implementation of reward policy, consult

> *Reward Management: A handbook of salary administration*, Second edition, Michael Armstrong and Helen Murlis, IPM and Kogan Page, 1988/90

or

> *Payment Systems and Productivity*, Angela Bowey, Richard Thorpe and Phil Hellier, MacMillan, 1986.

You will find a clear outline of the principles of job evaluation in

> *Job Evaluation: Objectives and methods*, Professor George Thomason, IPM 1980/85.

The general legal aspects of pay are dealt with in

> *Wages and the Law*, Keith Puttick, Richard Painter, Ian Henn and Stephen Evans, IPM and Shaw and Sons, 1989.

while the specific issue of deductions from pay is covered in

> *Cashless Pay and Deductions: Implications of the Wages Act 1986*, Eric Suter and Phil Long, IPM 1987.

Courses

Short courses and seminars on topics ranging from job evaluation to pensions and from performance related pay to varying the contract of employment, are offered by a number of reputable bodies, including the IPM, the British Institute of Management and many of the leading business schools.

Chapter Eight

Employee Relations

Introduction

Like any relationship, the employer-employee relationship can be either positive and constructive or negative and destructive. A large part of the work of the personnel department is concerned with making sure that the relationship works well for both parties.

This is done indirectly through every aspect of personnel work. The way recruitment and selection are handled, the quality of the training and development provided, the level and type of rewards available – can all contribute. Over and above this, there are a number of more direct ways in which the personnel department may seek to shape employee relations. These include:

- the employer's attitude towards trade unions (these are organizations set up to regulate the relationship between people working in a particular trade or industry and their employers) and the nature/quality of dealings with them;
- the methods adopted for dealing with employees whose conduct or work standards are causing difficulties (disciplinary procedures);
- the methods adopted for responding to employees' complaints or problems (grievance and disputes procedures);
- the methods adopted for controlling or reducing employment costs when changing working practices or falling demand for the organization's goods or services make this necessary (redundancy procedures);
- the quality and frequency of communications between employer and employees, and the extent of their involvement in decisions affecting them;
- the degree of concern shown by the employer for up-

holding employment rights, such as health and safety and equal opportunities.

What is Involved?

1. Trade Unions

If your organization is unionized, all the above items, as well as some of those discussed in earlier chapters, will be the subject of negotiation with trade union representatives, either nationally or locally. In a unionized environment, the personnel practitioner needs to understand:

- the aims and objectives of the union concerned. There is a common body of trade union belief – an ideology stretching back into the nineteenth century. This is based on the notion of collectivism, which we touched on in the last chapter, and the idea that only by acting together can employees prevent exploitation by their employers. But unions now differ markedly in the extent to which they believe employers and employees are bound to approach every issue from opposing sides. Some are now more concerned to use their collective strength to negotiate for the harmonization of pay and conditions for all employees and recognize that employers (or the managers who negotiate on the employer's behalf) and employees, share a common commitment to the success of the organization. Others remain convinced that the aims of management and unions must always conflict and that the objective of the bargaining process is to get the best deal possible for those they represent;
- the shape of the relevant negotiating machinery and how it operates. It is important to get to know the trade union representatives in the workplace, the shop stewards, and those who are full-time paid officials of the union regionally or nationally. It is also vital to get to know which has the most power and influence over the workforce;
- the legal framework of industrial relations. Powerful as many of them undoubtedly are, trade unions are democratic bodies set up to serve the needs of their

members. As such, they are required to hold properly conducted ballots before calling their members out on strike or taking other forms of industrial action. They are not allowed to victimize people who do not wish to join the union, and they must not use their power to force employers to break the law. Employers, too, have obligations under the law – to allow their employees to join a union and to give them reasonable time off to take part in union activities. As in most other fields of law, understanding the relevant acts of parliament will not be enough. It will be necessary to understand how the law has been applied in particular cases – a task made harder by the relative newness of much of the legislation;

- the content of any existing 'procedural' agreements between the employer and the union. These should include a grievance procedure, for handling complaints from individual employees; a disputes procedure, for dealing with complaints or problems raised by a group of union members; a disciplinary procedure, for dealing with management complaints about the conduct or performance of individual employees; a redundancy procedure, specifying how and on what conditions employees may be declared redundant and what steps must be taken to find alternative employment for those affected. The machinery for implementing the organization's policies on health and safety, equal opportunities and communication or the disclosure of information may also have been negotiated with the trade union(s);

- the 'case law' which has built up within the organization on the basis of such procedural agreements. Just as the written version of an act of parliament is only the starting point for judges to interpret how a law should be applied, so a procedural agreement provides only a framework for decision-making. Particularly in a hostile industrial relations climate, you will find that both sides can have long and very selective memories about how a particular procedure was implemented on a previous occasion;

- the content of current 'substantive' agreements. These are agreements about matters of substance, such as pay and conditions, rather than about procedural matters. Sometimes negotiators agree a phased settlement –

whereby part of a pay rise is paid on one date, part on another, or where management promise to deal with a particular issue again at a specified future date. The negotiator who goes to the negotiating table in ignorance of such agreements will soon regret this lack of preparation;

- management's attitude to the union. If you join a unionized company, you may initially get the impression that management and union representatives are uniformly hostile towards one another. Don't be misled into assuming that the way to curry favour with your boss is to score points off the union. Appearances can be deceptive. Underneath the bravado of negotiations and talk of macho management, the chief negotiators on both sides may be on the best of terms. Good industrial relations are not about point scoring. They are about trying to ensure that the legitimate aims of all those with a stake in the business – shareholders, management, clerical and professional staff and shop floor employees – are satisfactorily reconciled.

Such knowledge will help you in your day-to-day dealings with employees, whether or not you are personally involved in negotiating directly with union representatives. The more volatile the employee relations climate in your organization, the more important it will be that all the advice you give takes due account of the agreements which have been reached. If you *are* involved in direct negotiations, you will also need to acquire the skills to help you to do this successfully.

2. Disciplinary Matters

Employment law and good employee relations both dictate that performance problems are dealt with fairly and con-structively. Some employees may perform well for a long period and then commit one major transgression – like drinking too much at lunch time or 'borrowing' some money from the till. Some may always struggle to do their work to the required standard. Either way, it is in the interests of both employer and employee to resolve matters speedily and effectively and to re-establish a positive working relationship. You may be involved in

- drafting or revising disciplinary procedures. If there is a recognized trade union, the draft procedure will normally be a matter for negotiation. Otherwise, it may be introduced by management directly. The procedure should allow for a step-by-step approach. Minor offences will warrant only an informal warning, probably from a supervisor, when committed for the first time. A repetition, or a more serious offence, may lead to a formal warning from a manager, then a final warning and, in the last resort, dismissal.

  (If you are to be involved in drafting or revising a procedure, you will need a clear understanding of the rules of behaviour which apply in your organization, as well as a detailed knowledge of employment law;)
- helping to publicize the existence of the procedure and to train managers in its use. In some organizations, the mere idea of one day having to appear before an Industrial Tribunal to respond to a claim of unfair dismissal is enough to make managers lose all thought of trying to resolve a performance problem. In others, the identification of such a problem is seen to have only one possible outcome – and the employee will be sacked on the spot, without regard for the consequences.

  If you wish your line managers to understand what the law, and your disciplinary procedure, require, and if you want them to develop the skills needed to help 'problem employees' to become effective employees, you will need to spend time training them. They must understand that throrough investigation is always vital. This must include a full and constructive discussion of the employee's side of the story. In more serious situations, the employee will have the right to be accompanied by a colleague or trade union representative. Unless their transgression is very serious and there are no mitigating circumstances, employees should not normally be dismissed for a first offence. Instead, their line manager must be encouraged to provide them with help and support to put matters right;
- advising individual line managers on ways of handling specific cases. Consistency of treatment between employees is very important in disciplinary matters. For example, if employees are *sometimes* sacked for smoking

in prohibited areas – but not always – it may be difficult to show that a particular employee caught breaking the 'no smoking' rule knew what the consequences of this action would be. And unless you can *show* that he or she *did* know the consequences, an Industrial Tribunal may well take the view that you have acted unfairly in deciding to dismiss.

Line managers, most of whom will only encounter disciplinary problems occasionally, will expect you to be able to guide them through the application of the organization's own procedures and precedents and through both statute and case law. As well as having a knowledge of how Industrial Tribunals work, you will need to be familiar with the findings of the Employment Appeals Tribunal, the House of Lords, and the European Court of Justice when dealing with similar cases;

- exercising the authority to dismiss. Many employers have learnt the hard way that hasty or ill-conceived sackings can lead to bad feeling within the organization. If the employee chooses to take the case to an Industrial Tribunal, much management time will be taken up preparing to respond to the complaint. If the employee wins, the tribunal may order the employer to pay compensation and perhaps to re-engage or reinstate the employee.

  By vesting authority to dismiss in the hands of someone with detailed knowledge of employment law (usually the personnel manager), it should be possible to reduce the chances of people being dismissed for unfair reasons or in an unfair manner. (Not all organizations give personnel executive authority in disciplinary matters. In some, the managing director, or a general manager may be the only person who can take such a decision;)

- acting as a point of appeal. If a decision has been made to dismiss, or to apply some lesser sanction such as demotion or suspension, the employee should have the right of appeal. The appeals procedure should allow for a thorough and impartial review of the case. The panel is likely to be chaired by either the personnel director, or the managing director;

- recording and monitoring the progress of disciplinary cases. Each formal warning which an employee receives should be confirmed in writing. The employee should be asked to acknowledge receipt, perhaps by signing a copy of the letter. This should be kept on file for a reasonable length of time. The number and form of such warnings could be an issue in a tribunal hearing, so it is vital that they are carefully recorded and safely filed. If it has been agreed that specific action will be taken to help the employee, for example by providing extra training, further monitoring will be necessary to make sure that it has happened. And any board of directors which is interested in the quality of employee relations is likely to want a periodic report on the number and nature of disciplinary problems which have occurred. It will not be possible to provide this unless careful records have been kept.

3. Grievances and Disputes

Just as management will need, from time to time, to draw attention to problems relating to employee performance or conduct, so it is important that employees have an opportunity to voice their concerns about management action – or inaction. Unless they have a means of resolving the issues which concern them, employees may 'vote with their feet' by leaving the company altogether. Alternatively, they may withdraw their labour, either formally through strike action or informally by putting in less effort. You may be involved in

- drafting or revising a grievance procedure. This will set out the steps to be taken by individual employees who are unhappy about some aspect of their work or conditions of employment or about the way they are treated. You will need to be familiar with the structure of your own organization, as it is important that grievances should be referred upwards to the appropriate level of management and that appropriate time-scales are set for investigation and resolution;
- drafting or revising a disputes procedure. This will set out the procedure to be followed when a group of employees is dissatisfied with something relating to their work or conditions of employment or with the way one or more of their number are being treated. The procedure will need to clarify who is to be involved at each stage and what is

to be done in the event of failure to resolve the dispute. In a unionized environment it may be necessary to refer some disputes to what is known as arbitration – perhaps through the Advisory Conciliation and Arbitration Service (ACAS) – to obtain a decision which will be binding on both sides;

- helping to publicize the existence of the procedures, through written statements or briefing sessions. You may also need to train line managers in how to respond to complaints brought under these procedures, and in particular, how to conduct grievance interviews. They will need to recognize that a joint problem-solving approach will be much more use than an exhortation to 'cheer up and forget about it'. If the employees had felt they could do so, they would probably not have raised the grievance in the first place;

- advising individual employees or their representatives what they should do if they wish to lodge a complaint. Their first port of call will normally be their immediate boss;

- advising line managers on how to respond. Many managers will naturally feel defensive or hurt to think that they may have mishandled a situation or been unfair to an employee. They will need to recognize that such complaints are often the result of simple misunderstandings. Provided they are willing to explore the issue fully and openly, they may find what looked like a major problem has in fact provided the basis for building a more positive working relationship for the future;

- acting as a point of appeal if no solution can be found by line management. It is usually preferable for those hearing the appeal not to have been involved at earlier stages;

- recording and monitoring the progress of grievances and disputes and preparing periodic board reports indicating the number of each and the level at which they were settled.

4. Redundancies

In an ideal world, human resource planning would be so accurate, and workforces so flexible, that any change in the demand for numbers or skills would be accommodated without the need for the trauma of enforced redundancies. In the real world, where technological development and economic uncertainty are facts of life, few organizations can rule out all possibility that their demand for particular types of work will cease or diminish at some point. When it does, unless they can find suitable alternative employment for their people, they will be faced with redundancy. To cope with such an eventuality, you may be involved in

- drafting or revising a redundancy procedure. Because every job lost to an employer potentially represents a member lost to the trade union, you will find any changes you propose to make are a matter for debate. You would be well-advised to draft your policy in a way which makes it clear that redundancy is a last resort – after attempts have been made to reduce numbers through natural wastage, termination of temporary contracts, and voluntary redundancy.

  You will need to be familiar with the law relating to redundancy. This covers consultation with any recognized trade unions, notification to the secretary of state for employment, entitlement to redundancy payments, time off to look for alternative work, and trial periods in any alternative employment which the employer offers. It will also be necessary to define what will happen when it comes to selecting who is to be made redundant. This in turn requires a clear understanding of the circumstances in which selection for redundancy could be regarded as unfair and lead to a claim being taken to an Industrial Tribunal.

  Close consultation with union and line management will be necessary, to determine how the arrangements will work, and the terms on which redundancy will be offered or enforced. The law establishes only a minimum entitlement to redundancy pay – employers can be more generous, if they can afford it;
- helping to publicize the procedure. If, as is desirable, the revised procedure is being introduced at a time when no redundancies are envisaged, it may not be appropriate to make a big issue of any changes, for fear of arousing suspicions that cut backs are imminent. But it is important that everyone knows that there is a properly worked-out procedure, to protect them;

- advising the management on alternative ways of reducing employment costs. In many cases, the root cause of redundancy is the need to save money. The personnel manager can ask searching questions about the ultimate aim of the cut-back, and cost out alternative ways of meeting that objective. Sometimes it can be more expensive, at least in the short term, to let people go. The cost will include not only their redundancy pay but also their goodwill and their expertise. The organization may need both of these again before too long;
- taking part in notification or consultation arrangements. If more than ten employees at one establishment are to be made redundant within a thirty day period, the Department of Employment must be advised on Form HR1. The union, if there is one, must also be advised, whether or not those affected are actually union members. They must be given a chance to suggest how the situation should be dealt with;
- calculating entitlement to redundancy payments. This will often need to be done before anyone else is aware of the possibility of redundancy. Since the information you are asked to provide may be part of a costing exercise to help management to decide whether or not to proceed, it could be that the redundancies will not in fact take place.

  This is, therefore, one of the most highly confidential aspects of the work of the personnel department. When redundancy rumours are in the air, all it needs is a little careless talk from someone in personnel – who after all *must* know – and you could have a major employee relations problem on your hands.

  Working out redundancy entitlements also involves a painstaking set of calculations, as each employee's entitlement will relate to their length of service between particular ages, and to their current rate of pay. A pre-prepared table, (or computer programme) relating to the state scheme and/or your own company scheme, can save time and help reduce the chance that incorrect figures will be quoted. But the figures must always be double-checked. How would you feel if you were told you were losing your job but would receive £10,000 compensation – only to be called back next day to learn that the figure had shrunk to £5,000?
- notifying those affected. Everyone must be given due legal

notice of redundancy. If at all possible, it is better for those directly affected to be told personally rather than by letter. They will need to be advised of the effective date of redundancy, the reasons for it, the amount of any payment due and details of any action being taken to try to find alternative employment elsewhere in the organization.

If the numbers involved are large, this can mean a whole team of personnel staff being deployed to break the news and/or to advise people of their entitlements. People will react to the news in very different ways. Some may be literally devastated. Some will cry. Some will be angry or abusive. For the newcomer to personnel, the first encounter with the shock waves of a major redundancy can be a harrowing experience;

- counselling. After the initial shock, those who are to lose their jobs, and those who are to stay, will need help rebuilding their lives. It may be possible to offer alternative employment, elsewhere in the company or group. If so, the possibilities will need to be explored by personnel, and discussed with employees.

Financial advice, advice on how to set about looking for another job or starting a new career, perhaps on a self-employed basis, and personal counselling to help employees come to terms with their situation, may all be needed. Sometimes these can be provided by a specialist 'outplacement' consultancy. Sometimes the staff of the personnel department must manage as best they can.

Particular care may be needed in helping remaining employees to respond positively. Their feelings of relief at being spared may be soured by doubt and suspicion. Will there be further redundancies? What will life be like when the others have gone? Will they have to work twice as hard to make up? Unless sufficient attention is paid to these very understandable fears, the long-term implications for employee relations could be serious.

Nor may the personnel department itself be exempt from some of these problems. It takes a high standard of professionalism to counsel the management and staff of other departments through a large-scale redundancy. It takes an even higher standard when you know that the last

names on the redundancy list are likely to be those of the
personnel team;

- keeping accurate records of each case and of progress
  during the search for alternative employment. Senior
  management may wish to be kept up to date with how
  many people are being re-deployed. At the individual
  level, any subsequent allegations of unfair selection for
  redundancy can best be countered by showing that the
  agreed procedure was followed and that all that could have
  been done to find alternative employment, was done;

- liaising with payroll, pensions and other relevant departments to make sure that all termination payments come
  through on the due date. The normal administrative
  arrangements on termination of employment must not
  be overlooked. Staff uniforms, equipment, company cars
  and so forth must be collected. Holiday entitlements must
  be calculated, and P45's must be issued in the normal
  way.

5. Communications

Keeping employees in the dark is not a recipe for good
employee relations. Employees who invest skill and effort
in their organization have, arguably, just as much right to
know what is going on and to have a say in its affairs as
do financial shareholders. This need not mean bombarding
everyone with reams of closely typed reports. The *quality* of
communication, not the quantity, is what matters.

Some of this communication will be channelled through
trade unions where these are recognized. They have a legal
right to have certain business information disclosed to them.
They also have the right to be consulted on certain matters –
such as proposed redundancies and health and safety issues.
Some communication should go to employees direct, or
through their line managers.

Many different levels of communication are required.
These range from day-to-day discussions of how work
is to be done or is progressing, to presentations about
the future objectives and strategy of the organization as a
whole.

It is easy to assume that employees are only interested in

the things which will affect them directly in the short term. Indeed, line managers sometimes deliberately fail to pass on more 'global' information on the grounds that their people aren't interested or won't understand. Even if this is true, it could be a reflection as much on the manager's own style as on the intelligence and commitment of the people who work for them.

It is, of course, possible to subject people at any level in the organization to 'information over-load'. We all tend to retain information best when we can see how it relates to what we already know, and can work out what we should do as a consequence of it. Subjecting all employees to daily lists of figures telling them everything from how many orders have been received to how much it cost to get the windows cleaned – could be over-kill. But a carefully prepared, visually digestible summary of such information, professionally presented at appropriate intervals, might well give people a much stronger feel for what the business is all about. It could also help to motivate them towards increasing the orders and saving on the window cleaning bill.

In some ways, the work of the personnel department is *all* about communication. Every training session which is designed and delivered is communication. Every procedure discussed in this and previous chapters has to be 'publicized'. Every decision affecting an employee's pay or employment has to be 'notified'. Every aspect of employment practice has had to be discussed or negotiated. And every decision reached has to be properly recorded so that people can refer back to it later if need be.

There are, however, a number of more specific vehicles of communication which the personnel department may set up and manage. A few of those you may be involved in helping to compile are listed here.

Recruitment literature. This is sent to Jobcentres, schools and careers offices as well as to job applicants. It may take the form of a simple leaflet detailing job opportunities, or a glossy brochure complete with photographs and company history. Either way, the aim is to inform people what it will be like working for your organization and to give them an insight into the sort of opportunities you can offer.

Employee handbooks. These are issued to all employees when they join the organization. They provide a more 'user-friendly' statement of rules and procedures than the contract of employment, though it will usually be necessary to cross-refer to the contract. The handbook should explain how things work – like the sick pay scheme, holiday entitlements and what the organization expects of people in terms of rules of behaviour, time-keeping, dress and so forth.

Procedural manuals. Individual initiative is all very well, but does it really make sense for a hundred shop managers each to have their own way of handling a refund? Wherever there is one best way, or a way which must be adhered to for legal reasons or to tie in with other procedures, it will save time and increase efficiency if a standard system is introduced.

Those required to operate such systems must of course be trained in their use. But as the memory of their training fades, and systems are modified and revised, they will need some sort of reference manual to help them work out what to do in particular circumstances.

Among the procedures which may need to be codified in this way are those associated with employment. The personnel department will be responsible for compiling this section (and possibly some of the others). It will be for them to record, as clearly and concisely as possible, how individual managers should approach each aspect of their dealings with employees – from recruitment to disciplinary matters, and from pay to holiday rotas.

House magazines and newsletters. These are designed to increase employees' sense of belonging and their feeling of involvement in the affairs of the organization. The content of such publications is generally kept fairly light – this is not the vehicle through which to inform people of a change in their rate of pay or impending redundancy. Instead, it should focus on company and individual achievements. New products will be of interest to everyone if presented imaginatively and with conviction. New ideas and trends in the industry can also be featured, as can retirement awards, new recruits, and the exploits of the company skittles team.

Noticeboards. These can be used

(a) to provide up-to-the-minute information about forthcoming events;
(b) to give feedback on achievements to date – through the medium of sales graphs and output charts;
(c) as a permanent point of reference for employees, who are entitled, by law, to be able to consult particular documents, such as the organization's health and safety policy or particular sections of the Factories Act or the Office, Shops and Railway Premises Act;
(d) to notify employees of forthcoming opportunities, such as positions vacant.

Someone must take responsibility for ensuring that noticeboards are kept up to date and carry only authorized information. This may or may not include advertisements for secondhand cars and old lawn mowers. Unless the boards are checked and changed regularly they tend to become 'part of the furniture' and their impact as a communication vehicle will be lost.

Company briefings. The larger the organization, and the greater the distance between the boardroom and shop floor, the more important it is that there should be some sort of formal briefing system. This should ensure that everyone keeps abreast of company affairs and is made aware of the reasoning behind current strategy.

Some of this briefing can take place orally – perhaps using a 'cascade' system. This entails the board holding a large-scale meeting of senior people, at appropriate intervals during the year. The subjects covered can include performance in the year to date, budgets and plans for the remainder of the year, major strategic developments, and a chance for questions and answers on topics of concern. Once the senior team have been briefed, they in turn brief those who report to them – and so on, down the business.

Some of it will take place via written briefing notes, which are again passed down through the system. These can keep people informed about changes in organization structure, senior management appointments, and other issues. The content of the messages which are 'briefed' may sometimes come from line management. Responsibility for compiling and issuing briefing notes and for organizing board briefing meetings, often rests with personnel.

Suggestion schemes and quality circles. While much of the communication within organizations flows from the board downwards, there is much to be gained from encouraging as free an upward flow of information as possible. Employees, at all levels, may be encouraged to put forward their ideas on any aspect of life in the organization – from areas where money or time could be saved to ideas for new products or services.

The traditional vehicle for this is the suggestion scheme. Employees write their suggestions down, perhaps using a special card, and submit them to a panel of assessors. If, after appropriate investigation, it is considered that the suggestion will save or make money or bring about some tangible improvement, a cash award may be made to the employee. Sometimes this is linked to the amount of money the company is likely to make out of implementing the idea. The personnel department is usually involved in the administration of such schemes.

It may also have some involvement where ideas and suggestions are debated among the work group themselves, as part of a 'quality circle'. Here, each working group is encouraged to meet regularly to explore any factors which may be limiting output or quality and/or any savings or improvements which could be made. Many of the ideas which emerge are put into practice directly, by the work group themselves. Those with wider implications may go before a committee to be assessed.

Personnel may be involved in setting up such a scheme and monitoring its effectiveness. If the approach is to work, it may also be necessary to mount a very careful training programme, for the work groups and their supervisors, so that all can understand and come to terms with the thinking behind the scheme.

6. Upholding Employment Rights

All employees have the right to join or not to join a trade union, the right not to be unfairly dismissed, not to be subjected to racial or sexual discrimination, not to be exposed to unnecessary hazards, not to have unauthorized deductions made from their pay – and many more. The employer who rides roughshod over any of these rights will not enjoy the benefits of positive employee relations – and is breaking the law into the bargain.

It will be for the personnel department to ensure that practices in all these areas are of a high professional standard. This will involve:

- making sure all employees know what their rights are – in relation to everything from trade union membership to holiday entitlements – and training line managers to uphold these rights. This is not always easy. Some managers would prefer employees not to know that their contract gives them the right of appeal against dismissal or that it entitles them to an hour for lunch. While some feel they can 'get away with' doing less than the law demands, this is very shortsighted. People do not like being exploited. Good employee relations are built on understanding and trust, not ignorance and suspicion;

- establishing a positive commitment to equal opportunities. In Chapter Four we discussed the importance of adhering to the Sex Discrimination Act and the Race Relations Act. In Chapter Seven, the Equal Pay Act and Equal Value Regulations were mentioned. Positive employee relations demand that everyone who works for your organization (as well as everyone who would like to join you) really *does* have equal opportunities – to be trained, to contribute, to earn promotion, and to play a full part in the success of the undertaking.

  Personnel will be involved in drawing up an equal opportunities policy, and training managers in its implementation. They will also need to monitor its effectiveness, and examine the changing mix of employees at various levels in the organization. If all the low-paid and junior roles are filled by women and members of ethnic minorities, while the high-paid and senior jobs are filled by white men, this does not automatically prove that the organization discriminates unfairly. But it is food for thought and should provide the spur to positive action to help attract a different mix;

- making health and safety a way of life. Employees have a right to expect that their employer will do all that is 'reasonably practicable' to ensure their health and safety at work. The Health and Safety at Work Act specifically requires this. Employers who, through their 'consent, connivance or neglect' jeopardize the safety of their employees, may suffer heavy fines or even a prison sentence. They will also forfeit the confidence and commitment of their workforce.

  Personnel will be involved in designing health and safety policy and procedures, making sure that they draw upon the appropriate technical expertise in doing so. They should also train managers to help them see safety as an investment rather than as a cost, and train employees to help them do their jobs in the safest, rather than just the quickest, way. Personnel staff and line managers may also discuss health and safety matters with trade union representatives on a safety committee. They may devise safety campaigns and incentive schemes to encourage everyone to make safety a priority.

If and when accidents or cases of industrial disease do occur, these should be reported to the personnel department. Their task will then be to advise the insurance company, in the event of claims for compensation, ensure that the causes of the accident are fully investigated and that everything possible is done to prevent a recurrence. If the accident or illness results in absence from work for more than three days, personnel must notify the Health and Safety Executive on a special form. They may also wish to demonstrate their concern for the injured employee by visiting him or her, helping with any financial problems, and developing the sort of welfare role discussed in Chapter Nine.

The number of days' work lost through accidents, and the causes of accidents, must both be monitored closely. Trends should be noted for presentation to the board and inclusion in the company's annual report.

Large industrial organizations usually employ a specialist health and safety officer, who may report either to the personnel director or the manufacturing director. Even if the reporting channel is outside the personnel function in your organization, the importance of the link between health and safety and the broader field of employee relations means that you cannot divorce yourself completely from it. Furthermore, the personnel department, like every other working area, has its own hazards – from trailing telephone wires and unstable filing cabinets to overloaded sockets and heavy equipment.

Who Does What?

The personnel department can set up the machinery for good employee relations. They can establish negotiating structures and communication systems and install appropriate policies and procedures for dealing with redundancy, discipline, grievances, health and safety, equal opportunities and the rest. But they cannot make the machinery work without the positive and active co-operation of their line management colleagues and the workforce.

This cooperation does not just happen. It must be earned. Personnel cannot stand on the sidelines preaching unrealistic messages which don't square with the pressures of day-to-day life on the shop floor. Instead, they must get in there and prove that good employee relations – treating people as intelligent individuals, not as slavish 'factors of production' – makes sound commercial sense. This, in turn, may mean helping management and workforce to tune in to new concepts such as 'Just in Time', 'Total Quality and the 'empowerment of people' (for further reading, see page 142), in preference to more traditional assumptions about the way work is managed.

On a day-to-day basis, it will be for personnel to

- advise on the development of an employee relations policy which reflects legal requirements, good practice and organizational realities;
- establish workable procedures and machinery for implementing them;
- communicate and train others in their use;
- co-ordinate practice and precedent to ensure consistency thoughout the organization;
- take a lead in negotiating with trade unions;
- monitor the effectiveness of all aspects of employee relations policy.

It will be for line managers to

- contribute to the formulation of policy and procedures;
- manage the day-to-day communication with individual employees;
- implement employee relations policies and procedures;
- take part in negotiations affecting their people.

Who Can Help?

Employee relations is an area where a little knowledge can be dangerous. An ill-considered change in an employee's terms and conditions can lead to a claim for constructive dismissal. A paternalistic concern to 'protect' women from work which might prove too 'demanding' for them can lead to a sex discrimination case. An ill-timed comment about the company's future prospects can jeopardize the flow of union negotiations. The thoughtless handling of an employee injured at work can do untold damage to the morale of their colleagues.

Wherever possible, therefore, you should avoid being thrown in at the deep end in employee relations matters. Ideally, you should take the time to acquire an in-depth understanding of the legal and institutional framework of industrial relations.

Courses

Such knowledge can best come from the IPM professional education scheme, though study for the Certificate in Personnel Practice will provide a basic insight. If you need knowledge in a hurry, choose one of the short courses or touring workshops offered by the Institute or by other reputable bodies such as Croner Conferences or IRST (Industrial Relations Services Training).

Books

Many management texts can provide an insight into employee relations. For in-depth coverage of the theory and practice of industrial relations, try

A Textbook of Industrial Relations Management, George Thomason, IPM, 1984.

The legal background is well covered in

Essentials of Employment Law, Third edition, David Lewis, IPM, 1990.

For a practical guide to day-to-day industrial relations problems, have a look at

A Handbook of Industrial Relations Practice, Second edition, Brian Towers (ed), IPM and Kogan Page, 1987.

Some pointers to effective negotiating can be found in

Negotiation: Skills and strategies, Alan Fowler, IPM, 1990.

The specific problems associated with redundancy are dealt with in

Redundancy Counselling for Managers, Giles Burrows, IPM, 1985.

while

The Right to Dismiss, Second edition, M Whincup, Oxford, 1987.

will guide you through the complexities of dismissal.

A comprehensive guide to equal opportunities issues is

Equal Opportunities, The way ahead, Jane Straw, IPM, 1989.

For health and safety, try

Health and Safety at Work Act: A guide for managers, Richard Howells and Brenda Barrett, IPM, 1982.

If you are interested in the broad field of employee relations, you ought also to familiarize yourself with some of the issues relating to work organization which are discussed in

Japanese Manufacturing Techniques: Nine hidden lessons in simplicity, Richard J Schonberger, MacMillan, 1982.

and

Building a Chain of Customers, Richard J Schonberger, Hutchinson Business books, 1990.

These books include discussion of concepts such as Just in Time and Total Quality. To understand the thinking behind the move towards empowering people, read

Thriving on Chaos: Handbook for a management revolution, Tom Peters, MacMillan, 1988.

Chapter Nine

Employee Services

Introduction

As we saw in Chapter One, some employers hold firmly to the belief that adherence to minimum legal standards is all that it takes to discharge their obligations to their employees. Others have a more widely-based concern for the quality of people's working lives, and for the arrangements made to help them manage the boundaries between work and private life.

In this chapter, we recognize that the quality of the relationship between employer and employee is not only governed by the sort of formal and sometimes legalistic procedures described in Chapter Eight. It also depends on the extent to which employers are prepared to

- recognize and help deal with the stresses and strains of employees' lives – through providing personal counselling;
- ensure that their people have a healthy diet – through providing low-cost, nutritious meals in a well-run staff restaurant or canteen;
- help keep their people fit – through providing exercise and recreational facilities for employees' use;
- help keep their people healthy – through regular medical checks, private health care provision and health education and anti-smoking campaigns – and visit them when they are sick;
- contribute to the general well-being of their people – through free or subsidized hairdressing, chiropody and other personal services;
- help people with financial difficulties – through the provision of company loans;
- help people with particular problems – like ex-offenders, alcoholics, drug abusers and those who are HIV positive;

- help people through potentially difficult transitions – like returning to work after having a family, or preparing for retirement;
- say 'thank you' to people, not just for specific tasks but also for their loyalty and commitment – through long service awards and leaving gifts;
- contribute to the well-being of the local community – through allowing company facilities to be used by local residents or seconding staff to help with community projects.

These are just some of the services which an enlightened employer may provide – and which the personnel department may need to design and administer.

What is Involved?

1. Personal Counselling

Marital and family problems, housing difficulties, debts and work-related stress are no respecters of persons. People at any level, from top management to junior recruit, may find themselves distracted by or failing to cope with these and a whole raft of other such issues.

If you are moving into personnel in the hope of being able to help people resolve problems like these, you are not likely to be disappointed. The extent to which you will become directly involved will depend on

- your organization's attitude to welfare;
- whether or not there is a specialist welfare function within the personnel department;
- whether or not you are the kind of person in whom others are willing to confide.

The extent to which you are able to help people will depend on

- how effective a counsellor – rather than problem-solver – you can learn to be. Welfare counselling is not about solving other people's problems. It is about helping them to identify and think through alternative courses of action and to opt for the one which best meets their needs. Some will find your sympathetic understanding and willingness to listen will help them – on the basis that a 'trouble shared is a trouble halved'. But many will need more specific help;

- how expert you can become in recognizing when specialist help is needed – and where to find it. Medical, psychiatric, or social services, Citizens' Advice Bureaux, solicitors, undertakers, the Samaritans – from time to time your employees may have need of any or all of these.

You will need training in both these aspects if you are to make a real contribution. You will also need to be one hundred per cent discreet about *all* the problems that come your way.

2. Staff Canteens

Larger organizations, and those which are sited at a distance from cafes and restaurants, often offer on-site eating facilities to their workforce. Sometimes, these are staffed and managed by the company's own employees. Sometimes, they are operated by outside caterers on a contract basis. Either way, someone within the personnel department is likely to have a 'watching brief' over this particular service.

If the canteen is managed in-house, there will be catering staff to recruit and train, appropriate employment conditions to be determined and administered, and perhaps an additional union with which to negotiate. Even if contract caterers are used, someone must negotiate the contract and monitor the quality of the food and the standard of service. Whoever is responsible for this is unlikely to be short of eager advisers. Complaints about everything – from the temperature of the soup to the greenfly in the lettuce must be taken up and acted upon!

The staff canteen *can* be viewed simply as a necessary evil – a way of keeping people fed and of avoiding a mass exodus to the pub at lunchtime. More positively, it can become part of a wider healthcare programme, geared to improve physical fitness. Healthy eating – fruit, fresh vegetables and high fibre foods generally – can be offered. Over time, employees *may* be persuaded to trade in their pie and chips in favour of something less likely to shorten their life expectancy.

3. Exercise and Sports Facilities

The dangers of work-related stress and the benefits of regular exercise are becoming more thoroughly understood. Many British companies draw the line at the sort of corporate keep-fit sessions practised by some Japanese concerns. Nevertheless, the chance for people to 'work out', at the beginning, middle or end of the day, is an increasingly valued employee service. Although it is usually only larger organizations which can afford to provide such facilities on the premises, many others can negotiate special concessions at local gyms or fitness clubs.

Many British companies draw the line at the sort of corporate keep-fit sessions practised by some Japanese concerns

In a similar vein, some big companies still retain their own sports and social clubs for use by employees and their families. Works outings, sports days and family gatherings are less popular than they were – but still have a part to play in some organizations.

If yours is involved in providing any of these services, the management and/or administration may well be handled within the personnel department. This could mean anything from negotiating a cut-price rate for weight training at the local gym, to ordering the beer and leading the singing on the coach to Bognor!

4. Medical Facilities, Health Education and Sick Visits

The consequences of many potentially serious disorders, from heart disease to breast or cervical cancer in women, can be greatly reduced if they are detected early enough. Marks and Spencer is among the leading organizations which provides periodic health screening for employees, to pick up the early signs of such problems.

Many others offer private health care schemes, such as BUPA – either free or as part of a group scheme at reduced cost to employees. The availability of medical advice at the workplace, perhaps via a visiting local GP and/or professional nursing staff, is also a service to employees, although in some industries regular checks are required by law.

While such services clearly require qualified staff to handle the medical aspects, the management and administration may again fall to the personnel department. Much of this may again be highly confidential and will require the utmost discretion from all those involved.

Few people want to make themselves ill. Yet many persist in habits like smoking, excessive alcohol, poor diet – all of which will have an adverse effect on their health. Health education, to alert people to these dangers and help them learn how to avoid them, can be a relatively inexpensive way of improving the quality of their lives – and of saving literally hundreds of days 'off sick'.

If, in spite of all this, they do get sick, the caring employer will want to show his or her concern. The employee's boss and/or someone from the personnel department will be expected to maintain close contact with the employee and his or her family – particularly in cases of serious illness. Visits to the employee's home, help and support to the family, get well messages and gifts, may all form part of this aspect of the welfare role.

5. Personal Services

Employees who are at work all day may have little time to

spare to make themselves feel or look good. A hairdresser, a manicurist or a chiropodist on the premises could do wonders for morale, simply by devoting time and attention to employees' personal needs.

Someone must work out which of these services will be most valued by employees. Someone must recruit or hire in the services of appropriately trained staff. Someone must negotiate for a suitable room and associated equipment. Someone must decide who is eligible to use those services, when and how often. And someone must publicize and administer the service.

6. Company Loans

Some organizations offer this facility as a matter of course. Indeed, entitlement to a reduced rate mortgage or other such financial assistance is a key part of the employment package in the financial services sector. Others will only consider loans in extreme circumstances, where a member of staff is experiencing acute financial difficulties.

Either way, the decision as to how much, over what period and at what repayment and interest rates, must be carefully thought through. Keeping track of repayments received, chasing up outstanding balances – especially from employees who leave the company – and making sure the paperwork is in order – for Inland Revenue inspection if necessary – can be a full-time job.

7. Ex-offenders, Alcoholics, Drug Abusers and those who are HIV Positive

Some employers go through life assuming that none of their employees ever has been or ever will be touched by any of these – and that any potential recruits who have a history of such problems will be screened out during the selection process.

Such employers are deluding themselves. These four issues, and others related to them, are now so prevalent that sooner or later most employers are likely to encounter them. There are two possible responses:

- sack the person concerned, and stick your head back in the sand;

or

- provide help and counselling and an opportunity to contribute.

For a concerned employer, the first of these is not a serious option. The second, though, is often easier said than done. The counselling of those with drink, drugs or AIDS-related problems is *not* a job for a well-meaning amateur. Professional help is vital.

8. Women Returners and Creche Facilities

When time and effort have been spent training someone, it makes no sense to throw it all away just because she will be out of the workforce for a few years bringing up a family. Some employers now recognize this, and have set up schemes to encourage such women to return to them when they wish to resume their careers. Regular briefings and training sessions are held to keep the prospective returners in touch with what is happening in the organization and up-to-date with new developments in their work.

The return to work for such women will of course be quicker and easier if they can bring their children with them. New recruits, with no previous history of employment in the organization, will also be easier to attract if childcare facilities are available. For big employers, the setting up of their own workplace nursery may be a viable employee service. For those without the (considerable) resources required for this, joint action with other local employers can be the answer.

The initiative to set up such schemes, and their management and administration, are most likely to come from the personnel department. Careful research into the wishes and expectations of existing and potential employees should precede their introduction. The objectives must be clear from the start. If the aim is simply to tide the company over a period of labour shortages, there may be easier and more cost-effective ways of doing this. If, on the other hand, the aim is to develop a progressive and comprehensive employee services package, the costs will need to be weighed against the potential long-term benefits of a more committed workforce – of both sexes.

9. Retirement Preparation

An employer who is really concerned about the quality of people's working life will take this through to the end of the employment contract, and beyond. Instead of abruptly casting people adrift when they reach retirement age, the enlightened employer looks for ways of easing the transition. Pre-retirement financial advice can help people work out how best to invest the lump sum which the company pension scheme will pay out. Counselling can prepare them for some of the events, like bereavement, which they may have to face as they grow older.

A full scale pre-retirement course may be designed by the training department, using the services of in-house financial advisers and counsellors where appropriate. Alternatively, a number of specialist organizations offer this sort of facility on an individual company or shared basis.

Some people find that severing all links with the organization to which they may have devoted many years' service, is a painful process. The lead up to it can be made easier if a period of part-time working can be arranged before the final break. The period after it can be eased if pensioners are allowed to continue using company facilities, such as the staff canteen, and are invited to regular reunions, perhaps with their spouses.

All this takes careful planning and organizing by the personnel department, usually in close co-operation with the pensions department, if there is one.

10. Long-service Awards and Leaving Gifts

A tie pin or brooch at 25 years' service and a gold watch at 50 are, in some organizations, highly prized symbols of long and faithful service. Such awards will not compensate for shoddy treatment in other aspects of the employment relationship. But the organization which lets such momentous anniversaries pass without any form of recognition may well

Pensioners should be allowed to continue using company facilities

be seen as mean and unappreciative by its long-suffering workforce.

The chance of a cup of tea with the directors, and a photograph of the award ceremony in the company newspaper, can be an important ritual on such occasions. It is even more important when people leave after long service, particularly on retirement. How would you feel if you retired after 40 years with a company and no-one even bothered to say goodbye? It happens. But not in companies which value commitment.

Making sure it doesn't happen in your organization is yet another administrative burden for the personnel team to shoulder. It demands a system to signal the approach of anniversaries, retirements and other long-service milestones. It demands decisions regarding the form the awards are to take – vouchers, gifts or cash. Catering and rooming arrangements must be made and invitations sent to directors and other appropriate guests. A photographer may need to be booked, flowers ordered, and so on.

11. Community Relations

Most of the aspects of personnel work which we have discussed in this and previous chapters have to do with the organization's present workforce. But no organization exists in a vacuum. All are dependent on the world outside their gates. For the future, they will need a supply of skilled employees, a market for their product or service, and allies in lobbying local and central government about matters affecting their area or industry. To secure all of these, they need to foster their relations with the wider world.

Someone, therefore, must ensure that the social and environmental implications of the organization's activities are properly considered. Someone must take time to build positive and relevant education–industry links. Someone must try to ensure that the organization is seen as a positive force, not a negative one, in the community.

Ideally, that someone will be the chief executive. Certainly someone at board level must take direct responsibility for such issues. Because so many of them impinge upon the supply and retention of labour, though, that someone is sometimes the personnel director.

Hopefully he or she will not be left to pick up the pieces after careless talk has caused a health scare in the local population. Hopefully he or she will be able to take a proactive role in making sure that all employees see themselves as ambassadors for the company and that they will talk enthusiastically about its activities to those with whom they come in contact. Quite clearly this will not happen unless the organization has *earned* the right to expect it, through genuine concern for the quality of working life.

Nor should community relations consist solely of telling everyone how good you are. Your organization needs the community to flourish and prosper. You won't be in business without them. So progressive employers reach out to help the community, perhaps by sponsoring local projects or seconding people with appropriate expertise to help manage them.

Everyone in the personnel department will need to play their part in fostering this relationship. All their contacts with the outside world should contribute positively to it. These contacts are likely to be many and varied. They could include:

- visiting local schools and colleges to give careers talks or to service a stand at careers fairs;

- providing work experience and other placements for pupils or teachers as part of an education-industry link;
- helping final year pupils to present themselves effectively at interview, by running mock interviews and providing feedback to participants;
- liaising with other employers over the development of local initiatives – such as joint recruitment drives, transport arrangements or workplace nurseries;
- liaising with local and central government departments and agencies and with police, health and safety inspectors and the fire service.

Even when relaxing with friends in the organization, the personnel specialist needs to be aware of the potential impact of any negative comments they may make. Of course you will not always find yourself completely in tune with *everything* your organization does. But as a personnel professional you do have an obligation to try to understand *why* things have been done as they have, and to appreciate that the consequences of doing them differently, or not doing them at all, would have been even worse.

(Clearly if people in your organization are deliberately flouting the law and you have tried in vain to stop them, your loyalty to your profession will mean you must speak out, against the company. Fortunately such situations are rare.)

Who Does What?

The extent and nature of the provision of employee services is a policy decision. Like other such decisions, it must be taken with full knowledge of the costs and benefits which are likely to accrue. But it cannot be taken only on the basis of short-term cost-benefit analysis. The employer who *does* provide the sort of services discussed in this chapter will do so because of a fundamental belief in the dignity of human labour and the long-term value of a committed workforce.

Once the board have determined which services will be offered, and to whom, most of the day-to-day management and administration will fall to the personnel department. The main exceptions may be in the area of personal counselling, where line managers may feel that the initial responsibility rests with them. Where this happens, the chance to build a positive, all-round boss–employee relationship will usually be a good thing. The only danger is that boss and subordinate may get so close to the problem that both may lose sight of its real implications.

In addition, services such as sick visiting and the presentation of long service awards may be more highly valued by the employee if a manager who knows them personally is involved. Wherever possible, line management should be seen to 'own' such activities. This lets employees know that these are not personnel department 'add-ons', but a genuine reflection of management concern for the well-being of employees.

Many of the other areas we have discussed require the services of people who are specialists in their own right. Medical practitioners or occupational health specialists, legal advisers, professional caterers and the like, all have their part to play. In a large and sophisticated organization, where all these skills are retained in-house, they may come together only at the top. So the heads of each of these employee service functions may report in to the personnel director. Below board level, they should liaise and exchange information with other members of the personnel team, as appropriate.

In a small organization, where the personnel practitioner must be the Jack or Jill of all trades, whatever employee services are to be provided must be their responsibility. Line managers will look to the personnel department to:

- advise on which services are to be offered;
- design appropriate systems and/or bring in appropriate expertise;
- manage the process, including negotiating fees and the basis on which specific services are to be made available;
- administer the process, making sure all the planning, paperwork and any necessary payments take place in due time and form;
- monitor each service to maintain standards and ensure that each continues to be valued by employees as part of the overall employment relationship.

Who Can Help?

To keep abreast of current developments in employee services, consult the IPM magazine *Personnel Management*. This carries features and advertising which include the broad range of issues discussed in this chapter. For an indication of the services offered by other employers, you will also find Incomes Data Services publications provide a useful guide.

To develop the expertise needed to handle particular aspects of employee services, you will need specialist training. Counselling skills, particularly, are of value to all personnel practitioners, whether or not welfare specialists are available. An introduction to this type of interview is included in some general interview skills courses, such as the IPM short course on interview skills.

Books

To find out more about counselling and how to use it, consult

Counselling: A practical guide for employers, Michael Megranahan, IPM, 1989.

For an insight into the particular problems associated with drink and drug abuse, and some practical advice on how to draw up policies to deal with them, try

Drink and Drugs at Work: The consuming problem, Fred Dickenson, IPM, 1988.

If you need to know more about healthcare at work, you will find much useful information about how to construct and maintain a cost-effective programme in

The Corporate Healthcare Revolution: Strategies for preventive medicine at work, David Ashton, IPM/Kogan Page, 1989.

For help in developing your approach to liaising with education the IPM Training and Development Department have produced a

School/Work Liaison Workshop Package.

For a full and up-to-date list of providers of employee services, refer to the most recent annual edition of

Human Resource Management Yearbook, edited by Michael Armstrong, Kogan Page.

Chapter Ten

The Way Ahead – For Personnel and for You

Introduction

The work of the personnel department does not stand still. Within each of the specialist areas discussed in earlier chapters, and in the function as a whole, changes in the economic and political environment, employment law and technology make sure of that.

In this final chapter we will explore some of the issues which may influence the direction in which personnel work continues to develop. Then, if you are still interested in getting into personnel, there is some advice on how to go about it.

'Thriving on Chaos'

Much of the work of the personnel department is, as we have seen, concerned with establishing policies and procedures to ensure fairness and consistency of treatment for employees. Indeed, the impression given by some personnel departments is that they are the last bastions of system and order, holding firm against the whims and inconsistencies of line managers. The heading of this section, therefore, needs some explanation.

It comes from the title of a book by the American management guru, Tom Peters. Throughout the 1980s, Peters went 'in search of excellence' (the title of another of his books). He observed, discussed and analysed the way the world's most successful organizations operate. And he came to the conclusion that system, order and bureaucracy are not what successful management is all about.

Instead, flexibility, adaptability and perpetual change are what matter. Only those organizations which thrive on this, and set themselves up to use change as a positive driving force, can really meet the challenges of the 1990s.

If you read *Thriving on Chaos*, you could be forgiven for thinking that the days of the personnel specialist are numbered. Among Peters' 'prescriptions for a world turned upside down' are:

- abolish job descriptions
- forget job evaluation
- abandon your manuals and rule books, or cut them drastically
- don't let personnel people do your recruiting
- don't use psychological tests
- make training a line management responsibility
- make sure any personnel staff you have are based in the field rather than in head office
- simplify the structure of the organization, reduce the number of management levels, and involve everyone in everything.

Does this spell the end of personnel management as a specialist management function? It seems unlikely, not only because many remain sceptical of the value of Peters' prescriptions but also because the prescriptions themselves are not incompatible with the continuing development of personnel.

Peters' emphasis on line management responsibility for recruitment, training, reward and so on is in fact quite easy to reconcile with the approach to personnel management adopted in many organizations and described in earlier chapters.

It never has been a personnel department responsibility to make decisions *for* line managers. Personnel's task has been to work *with* line managers.

It never has been appropriate for personnel to devise systems and procedures which suit their *own* convenience, regardless of the pain and frustration they cause line managers. Their task has always been to work backwards from line managers' needs – for a fairer payment system or more effective selection decisions, and to find ways of accomplishing these ends as simply as possible. If rigid job descriptions and inflexible job evaluation systems fail to reflect the value system of the organization, no-one should advocate their continued use.

And it never has been appropriate for personnel to divorce themselves from the rest of the organization and expect the rest of the world to revolve around them. Their role has always been to help line managers examine and assess the human resource needs of the business, and to find ways of meeting them. You don't do that sitting in a plush office in HQ. You do it by getting out and talking to people, the people who do the real work in your organization. Then you examine what they tell you, in the context of the law and good employment practice, and work with line managers to develop approaches which move the organization forward rather than holding it back.

This is not to deny that Tom Peters' work has, and will continue to have, a profound impact – and a mainly positive one. Peters addresses himself to chief executives, not to personnel practitioners. This is important. It means that now, more than ever before, the management of people at work is at the top of the line management agenda.

Where the personnel department is seen as obstructive and bureaucratic, it may be swept away, or relegated to a purely administrative role. But where its members are seen as pushing the organization towards the best possible ways of managing the human resource, their contribution will be highly regarded and sought after.

Their priorities may well change. We will discuss these shortly. In many organizations, their job titles have already changed. What was once the staff department, then the personnel department, is now the human resources department. The thinking involved in this change – from personnel to human resources – bears closer examination.

Personnel versus Human Resource Management

As we saw in Chapter One, the term 'human resource management' implies thinking about people as an investment rather than as a cost, a resource which can increase an organization's competitive advantage rather than an overhead which reduces its profit.

For many personnel specialists, this is not a new idea. We have always felt that people ought to be valued as an asset, not simply controlled as a cost. What is new is that now line managers are sharing this view and have coined a new name to put some distance between it and their traditional view of personnel.

The implications of the switch to human resource management, however, go deeper and wider than this. Some of the strands which can be traced running through it are outlined below.

- The term 'human resources' is not synonymous with 'employees'. For some time, many organizations have been looking at new forms of work – from job sharing to home-working – and new types of contract – from executive 'temps' to annual hours. This represents a much wider *resource* than the traditional full-time permanent pool of contractual employees.
- 'Personnel' has never fully shaken off its 'do-gooding', welfare image. It has always been seen, at least partly, as having the interests of the workforce at heart – sometimes when the rest of the management team did not. Human resource management, on the other hand, is clearly identified with management's interests, and with the efficient running of the business. This is summed up by Lesley Mackay and Derek Torrington:

  'Underpinning personnel management are the twin ideas that employees need looking after while at work and that they are only effective when their needs are being met. Underpinning human resources management is the belief that getting the deployment of the correct numbers and skills at the right place is more important than patronizing involvement with people's personal affairs.' (From: The Changing Nature of Personnel Management, *IPM, 1986.)*

- Following from this, personnel managers, particularly in the 1970s, spent a lot of time heading off trade union problems. The more clinical human resource manager of the 1990s will spend time on planning, monitoring and controlling, rather than problem-solving and firefighting.

'Personnel' has never fully shaken off its 'do-gooding' welfare image

- To think in terms of 'human resources' is to think strategically about the use of resources to achieve objectives. The new label implies that 'people policies' will be clearly linked to the goals of the organization and tailored to suit its culture, in a way that perhaps the old label did not.
- 'Personnel', 'staff' or 'labour' are all terms which fail to do justice to the capabilities which people possess. 'Human resources', on the other hand, implies that 'resourcefulness' is one of the things which people bring with them to their work. The new label therefore conjures up a much more rounded view of the contribution which people can make.
- Part of the new thinking is that *all* the resources of the organization need to be brought to bear to ensure success. This implies that all the people in the organization must work together towards common goals. Much traditional personnel management has been geared towards handling the sort of industrial relations conflict which arises when the goals of management and workers diverge. The human resource manager will, the implication is, be working in a world where such conflicts are rare – because the talents

of each individual are being developed and used to the full, and because the old divisive terms and conditions of employment have been harmonized to produce one cohesive and fully committed workforce.

These six strands of human resource management do not add up to a nice neat package. There are potentially conflicting elements within it. But together they point the way in which the role of the personnel specialist is likely to develop.

Priorities for the Nineties

Whatever else happens during the 1990s, this *should* be the decade when personnel and line managers really do work together to ensure the success of their organizations. Personnel specialists will need to make certain that every aspect of personnel policy is fully compatible with the goals of the organization, and forms part of a coherent package. This will not be easy, given the context in which we will be operating.

Organizations will need to get to grips with four main issues:

- customer care. Recognition that the 'customer is king' dawned in the 1980s, and owes much to the work of Tom Peters. But improving customer care while combating high labour turnover, skill shortages and instability, will demand imagination and effort;
- the 'green' revolution. The drive for environmentally friendly products started in the 1980s but is gaining momentum in the 1990s. Developing new, ecologically safe products and marketing them to a public which is not nearly so gullible as in the early days of television advertising, will demand considerable creative talent – and a careful balancing of the costs of going green against the consequences of not doing so;
- information technology. The development of ever more versatile and user-friendly personal computers and related office technology is likely to force a rethink of some middle-management roles. They will need to spend less

time policing and checking the work of their subordinates, and more time acting as guide and mentor.
- the opportunities presented by the removal of trade barriers within Europe. These opportunities work both ways – enabling export markets to expand while at the same time opening up the home market to increased competition. The need for talented, multi-lingual entrepreneurs, ready and able to make the most of the challenge, could force a rethink of traditional career structures.

Such major developments will present a real challenge to the human resource specialist. They will force us to focus on

- training – for newly recruited staff, perhaps from non-traditional sources, who may lack the education or experience which might have been demanded in the 1980s;
- training – for everyone, to help them understand that the customer really is king – and that what they do on their assembly line or tucked away in their office, has a direct bearing on how the customer perceives the organization;
- training – for all those whose technical skills must be updated, to help them contribute fully to the development of new products and services for an ever more demanding market place;
- training – for all those who made a new year's resolution to become more computer literate in 1980 – and still haven't done it;
- training – for everyone who will be in contact with new customers in new markets – language training and cultural awareness will be high priorities here;
- training – for everyone who will be affected by or can contribute to the changes in individual roles or overall organization culture which these new priorities bring.

For all these reasons, training is likely to be at the forefront of personnel agendas in the 1990s. And, just in case the pressure from within the organization is not enough, the government may add further impetus by requiring all employees under 18 to study for a vocational qualification and/or by specifying a required period of off-job training for everyone.

None of this can be taken as read, though. Every training

specialist, in every organization, will need to analyse the extent to which these generalized priorities really apply to them. Training needs must be identified, objectives clarified, programmes designed and delivered using new training technologies and with maximum involvement from line managers – who themselves will need to be trained to train or coach their own people.

Important though training will be, it will not be the only priority for personnel. Among the others will be

- recruitment – of women returners, members of ethnic minorities, those who took early retirement in the 1980s, and indeed from any pool of trainable talent whose members can be wooed with offers of creche facilities, job sharing, transport to work or flexible hours.

This is already happening. Over the next few years line management is likely to look to their personnel specialists to try out as many 'new' forms of contractual arrangement as they can think of – from annual hours and term-time contracts to extended maternity and/or paternity leave, homeworking or teleworking.

Others will seize the opportunities to recruit from a much wider labour market. Some local authorities have already broken through national boundaries to recruit teachers from abroad when shortages make local recruitment impossible. After 1992, with the removal of trade barriers in Europe, we will be able to define the 'UK' labour market much more broadly. Migrant workers, and temporary secondments from other EC countries could become commonplace.

While all this is putting employers in general and personnel specialists in particular under pressure, there is always the likelihood that other more traditional pressures will reappear.

- Industrial relations – which languished in an uneasy calm for much of the 1980s – could re-emerge as a key issue in sectors where skill shortages add weight to union bargaining power.
- Payment systems – which are never far from the personnel agenda – will remain a key issue, as organizations look for more innovative and effective ways of rewarding and

retaining people with sought-after skills. We are likely to
see a move away from standard systems of evaluating *jobs*
towards more flexible payment for *skills*.
- The European Community Social Contract could provide
the impetus for new moves on health and safety, holidays,
rest periods, hours of work and equal treatment for men
and women.

Developments are likely, too, in the *way* personnel departments operate. More advanced computerized personnel
information systems will mean that many of the time-
intensive routines associated with personnel administration
are speeded up or eliminated. As the overall standard of
management information continues to improve, personnel
staff will be expected to have facts and figures at their finger-
tips – and the know-how to interpret and act on them.

If you are thinking about moving into personnel, one thing
is clear – you will not be short of challenges! Some ideas to
help you enter are given in the next section.

How to Get into Personnel

If you have studied the first nine chapters of this book, you
should be in a position to decide whether the work of the
personnel department is the sort of work you would like to
do. The next task is to determine whether you have 'got
what it takes' to get into personnel, and to decide on the
most appropriate route to follow.

The skills you will need

The precise personnel specification will depend on the
industry, the employer and the level and nature of the role.
The skills listed in Chapter One will provide an essential
starting point. In addition to the interpersonal, analytical
communication and creative skills listed there, you will need

- to present yourself as someone who can maintain the
professional integrity of the personnel department. Inveter-
ate gossips need not apply;

- a reasonable standard of numeracy. Don't be misled into thinking that 'being good with people' is all that is required. Numerical data – from labour turnover statistics to the canteen budget – will play a significant part in your life in personnel;
- some respect for authority. As a personnel practitioner, you will be expected to conform to, and help establish, the norms of the organization. You need to be accepted as a part of its management team – not as a fringe activity with its own rules of behaviour;
- the ability to look at things from an employer's perspective, rather than a purely personal one. Rightly or wrongly, many employers would look askance at prospective personnel practitioners who boasted of having stood up *too* vociferously for their individual rights. So if you did take your last employer to an Industrial Tribunal and win, don't expect all employers to regard this as a high commendation. Similarly, personnel management is not the most highly-paid management function. Even if it were, you would still be likely to find yourself recruiting, training, and administering pay and conditions for people who are paid more than you are. If you are the sort of person who will waste hours pondering the injustice of that, you will not be happy in personnel.
- some commercial awareness. Personnel departments do not provide a refuge from the presssures of the business world. They may not generally be charged with *making* money. But they are certainly required to use their own resources cost-effectively, and to make sure all their decisions take account of commercial reality as well as professional ideals;
- a tolerance of ambiguity. While many line managers have one boss and one set of inter-related objectives, personnel practitioners may often feel themselves pulled in conflicting directions. Changing business priorities, or the differing needs of different parts of the same business, mean that 'once and for all' decision-making is not always possible. This creates uncertainties which some people find worrying;
- the ability to derive satisfaction from working towards a goal – rather than from the immediate knowledge of

results. If you are the sort of person who needs to go home at night secure in the knowledge that your day's efforts have 'put money in the till' or 'beaten last year's figures', you may find personnel work frustrating. The results of your labours will often take quite some time to become apparent – and when they do, you may not get the credit for them;
- the ability to derive satisfaction from influencing events rather than direct decision-making. If you are the sort of person who is happiest making on-the-spot decisions and directing others, you could find it hard to adapt to a function which requires more subtle means of getting things done.

But if you

- have found the subjects discussed in earlier chapters interesting and challenging,
- feel you have or could acquire the necessary skills and knowledge, and
- genuinely want to help organizations and their people develop and grow,

you will find personnel management one of the most satisfying careers you could choose.

Routes into Personnel

Relatively few people start and end their careers in personnel. Most have worked in other functions before transferring into a personnel role. Sometimes, this is because personnel was not their first choice of career. Often, it is because entering personnel direct from school or higher education is not easy.

Many employers feel that maturity and 'experience of life' add to the credibility of people in personnel, and that an understanding of the reality of work in an organization is best gained through experience 'at the sharp end'. Personnel is certainly not the sort of career where you are 'too old at 25'. It *is* possible to get in at a clerical level direct from school or college. But if your sights are set on a more senior role you may need to be prepared to gain wider experience before specializing.

School leavers. Your chances of getting into personnel direct from school or college will be greater if you have office practice or secretarial skills. You may be lucky and see a junior clerical or secretarial post advertised, and get in that way. Much of your work will probably centre on the maintenance of the personnel information system, inputting data to the computer, filing, typing or word processing letters and contracts, and dealing with telephone queries.

If you show promise at this level, your employer may decide to give you day release to attend a Certificate in Personnel Practice course so that you can start to climb the professional ladder. Alternatively, you may be able to do the course in your own time.

If you have 'A' levels, you could join an 'A' level training scheme. Such schemes are offered by many large employers, but very few offer a direct route into personnel. Most are designed mainly to train and develop the organization's next generation of line managers. Once you are in employment, though, the organization's policy of promotion from within could mean that you are able to move into personnel if a vacancy occurs. If such an opportunity arises, you could increase your chances of selection by studying for either a Certificate in Personnel Practice or the IPM Professional Education Scheme, see page 171.

One word of advice. If you decide to go down this route, do it on the basis that it will give you a chance to explore a number of different business functions. It may be that your original desire to work in personnel will be confirmed during your training – or it may be that you will be drawn to something quite different. You are more likely to enjoy and benefit from your training if you approach it with an open mind, and your employers are more likely to feel that they have recruited someone with wide-ranging potential for the business.

If all this sounds a bit 'hit and miss', you can increase your chances of being able to move directly into personnel by obtaining more specific qualifications before looking for a job.

Graduates. About half the work of the personnel department
is done by people with degree level qualifications. This seems
likely to increase in future.

If your ultimate goal is definitely personnel management,
choose a business studies degree course which offers personnel
options and provides the opportunity for plenty of work
experience on company placements. A few such courses place
enough emphasis on the skills and knowledge of personnel
management for their graduates to be exempt from the IPM's
own professional examinations. The Institute only grants such
exemption where its Education Committee is satisfied that
students will spend at least part of their placement period in
a personnel department. Those who do this successfully quite
often find that the employer with whom they undertook a
placement offers them a job when they graduate.

Most business studies degrees aim to equip people for a
wide range of business activities and their graduates do not
qualify for IPM exemption. You may find, once you have
started the course, that you enjoy some other aspects more
than the personnel elements. If, however, your interest in
personnel is confirmed by the course, you could go on to
study for the IPM examinations on a full-time, part-time or
distance learning basis afterwards, and may be granted some
exemptions by virtue of your degree.

Business studies are by no means the only degree courses
which can lead to a career in personnel. A law or behavioural
science degree will teach much that is relevant to the work
of the personnel department. And many graduate recruiters
are less interested in the subject of your degree than in the
skills you have acquired and your potential for meeting the
demands of work in their organization.

Even so, relatively few employers recruit graduates directly
into their personnel departments. (You can identify those who
do from their entries in the graduate careers directories.)
Rather more offer a general management training scheme,
from which you *may* be able to progress into personnel.

If you apply to join such a scheme, you will need to assess,
at interview, what the chances of your moving into personnel
really are. If you are offered a place, you should only accept if
you are prepared to see the training through and, if necessary,
make a contribution to other functions besides personnel.

You will find there is a lot to be gained from learning about how the organization works and the different jobs which are performed within it. If you eventually do move into personnel, you will have a much clearer idea of the conditions under which people are working and their reactions to them. You will also be a lot less likely to become an 'ivory tower' personnel person – good at coming up with intellectually pleasing ideas, but hopeless at actually installing workable solutions.

Furthermore, if you have aspirations to reach the very top, you are more likely to do so if you are seen to have a wide-ranging understanding of the business and its objectives. If you restrict yourself to a particular specialism too early, you will reduce the chances of this.

If you still feel that you would like to gain direct entry to personnel after you graduate, your best hope is to equip yourself with some additional skills. Postgraduate secretarial skills will open up the possibility of becoming secretary to a senior personnel practitioner – and you can seek professional qualification from there. Alternatively, in smaller organizations, it is often the managing director's secretary who handles most personnel matters – and becomes the lynch pin of the organization.

The other main route will be to apply for a one-year postgraduate course in personnel management, and qualify for IPM membership.

IPM Professional Education Scheme. As most course tutors will confirm, even graduate membership of the Institute will not guarantee you entry to the profession. Those who graduate from full-time courses without any work experience often encounter considerable difficulty in finding jobs in personnel.

This frustrating 'Catch-22': no experience – no job; no job – no experience, is more likely to be broken if your course allows for a significant block of time to be spent on placement with an employer. If you can make enough impact during your placement, the least you will come away with is a first class reference. If a vacancy comes up shortly afterwards, you might also have a job.

If you are thinking of taking this route, ask the course tutor to tell you how long it generally takes for students to find personnel jobs afterwards – and what the college does to help. Of course your own initiative and marketability will be the prime determinants of how long it takes *you*. But a college which has a well-structured placement system, and a careers service or course tutor geared up to put you in touch with local employers, can give you a head start.

Obtaining the funding to undertake a full-time course can prove a major stumbling block. Most do not attract local education authority funding (although those who have had less than three years' grant previously may qualify for a discretionary award). Economic and Social Science Research Council bursaries are very hard to come by. So if you cannot fund the course yourself – perhaps with the aid of a bank loan – you may need to take a job outside personnel and study part-time instead.

This in many ways is the hardest option of all. You have to face all the stresses and strains of college attendance, assignments, reports and examinations on top of a full day's work. And you will find many of the work-related assignments hard to complete because you don't have direct access to a personnel department. For the same reason, you may find some of the topics discussed are harder to grasp and your contribution to class discussions is restricted because you can't relate them back to your own experience.

Employees in other functions. You may at present be working in public administration, teaching, engineering, or a secretarial or administrative role. Your work may bring you into contact with personnel policies and procedures – but you are not part of the personnel department. How do you get in?

If you work for a large employer with a progressive approach to career development, you may be able to persuade the personnel manager that you have a contribution to make. If you have shown the appropriate blend of skills in your present job, and perhaps added to this by studying for the IPM examinations in your own time, you should stand a chance of at least being interviewed when a vacancy arises at an appropriate level.

For many, though, the only way to break out of the current mould will be to change employers – usually via a full-time course. Be prepared to go back into the same industry afterwards – because then prospective employers will know that your previous work experience should enable you to understand their business fairly quickly. Be prepared to start at a level and salary lower than the one you left behind. And be prepared to construct the sort of curriculum vitae which really brings out the sort of competences you have developed – rather than just the jobs you have done.

Who Can Help?

Careers Advice

Local Education Authority and college/university careers services may be able to help you identify employers who are willing to train personnel specialists. They should also be able to help you to prepare a curriculum vitae which highlights your capabilities and potential.

The major careers directories, such as *Directory of Opportunities for Graduates; Graduate Opportunities* and *The Job Book*, should also help you to track down employers who have openings in personnel.

Job Advertisements

The Institute of Personnel Management produces two monthly publications – *Personnel Management* and *Personnel Management Plus*. These are by far the best sources of advertisements for personnel jobs. They are available free to all grades of member of the Institute and on subscription to non-members.

If you are trying to gain entry at clerical or secretarial level, scour the 'situations vacant' columns of your local paper. Employers don't always highlight the fact that the job is in personnel, but it may be there in the small print. Alternatively, register with a local employment agency and make it clear that you would like to be considered for any jobs in personnel.

Courses

Your best source of advice on courses in personnel management is the Institute of Personnel Management. Their

Education Department will send you details of the Professional Education Scheme and of colleges offering

- the one-year part-time Certificate in Personnel Practice – for which no formal academic qualifications are required;
- the Professional Education Scheme – which requires a minimum of five GCSE passes, at least two at 'A' level, or at least two years' relevant work experience. The course takes one year full-time and two or three years part-time and may lead to a postgraduate or polytechnic diploma as well as graduate membership of the Institute.

For details of short introductory courses, including a general introduction to the work of the personnel department, and for short courses to develop specific skills, contact the Institute's Training Services Department.

Remember

If you can't find work in a personnel department straight away, look for a job with some personnel content, however small. When you are ready to move on, the fact that you can say you recruited or trained your own staff, or were responsible for decisions affecting their pay or their future development, will do you no harm at all.

Good Luck!

General Reading

If you do decide to pursue a career in personnel management, you can follow up on the issues raised here by referring to:

Success in Management: Personnel, Third edition, Penny Hackett, John Murray, 1990.

If you enroll on an IPM course, your tutors will recommend that you study

Personnel Management: A new approach, Derek Torrington and Laura Hall, Prentice Hall and IPM, 1988.

and/or

A Textbook of Human Resource Management, Professor George Thomason, IPM, 1988,

as well as texts dealing in depth with particular specialist areas. Most of these are published by or in association with the IPM, who can supply a detailed book catalogue on request.

If you are in the position of having to set up your own personnel department in a small organization, you may need to establish your own reference library and to identify consultants and other sources of help and advice.

Some books which will help include:

the current edition of *Human Resource Management Yearbook*, Michael Armstrong, Kogan Page

and

Choosing and Using Management Consultants, Roger Bennett, Kogan Page, 1990.

To help you to ensure that you operate in accordance with professional standards, ask the IPM for a set of their codes of practice. These are available free from the Development Department at IPM, on receipt of a stamped addressed envelope. They cover a wide range of topics, from human resource planning to occupational testing.

For more detailed legal advice, take out a subscription to a regularly up–dated reference book such as

Croner's Reference Book for Employers, available from Croner Publications, 173 Kingston Road, New Malden, Surrey, KT3 3SS.

Useful Addresses

Advisory, Conciliation &
Arbitration Services (ACAS)
Head Office
27 Wilton Street
London SW1X 7AZ
Tel: 071-210 3000

British Association for
Commercial and Industrial
Education (BACIE)
16 Park Crescent
London W1N 4AP
Tel: 071-635 5351

British Institute of
Management (BIM)
Management House
Cottingham Road
Corby
Northants NN17 1TT
Tel: 0536 204222

Confederation of British
Industry (CBI)
London Office
Centre Point
103 New Oxford Street
London WC1A 1DU
Tel: 071-379 7400

Commission for Racial
Equality (CRE)
Elliot House
Allington Street
London SW1E 5EH
Tel: 071-828 7022

Department of Employment
Caxton House
Tothill Street
London SW1H 9NF
Tel: 071-273 3000

Department of Employment
(Scotland)
Cheshire House West
502 Gorgie Road
Edinburgh EH11 3YH
Tel: 031 443 8731

Department of Social Security
Hannibal House
Elephant and Castle
London SE1 6TE
Tel: 071-972 2000

Equal Opportunities
Commission
Overseas House
Quay Street
Manchester M3 3HN
Tel: 061 833 9244

Incomes Data Services (IDS)
193 St John Street
London EC1V 4LS
Tel: 071-250 3434

Industrial Society
3 Carlton House Terrace
London SW19 5DG
Tel: 071-839 4300

Institute of Manpower Studies
University of Sussex
Falmer
Brighton
Sussex BN1 9RF
Tel: 0273 686751

Institute of Personnel
Management
IPM House
Camp Road
Wimbledon
London SW19 4UX

Institute of Training and
Development
Marlow House
Institute Road
Marlow
Bucks SL7 1BN
Tel: 0628 890123

Training Agency
Moorfoot
Sheffield S1 4PQ
Tel: 0742 703342

Glossary

Advisory Conciliation and Arbitration Service (ACAS): an independent body which provides advice on employment matters and helps to bring together the parties to disputes.

Assessment Centre: a series of activities used in selection and management development to simulate parts of the job to be filled, observed by a team of trained assessors.

Audit (role): one in which the personnel department is responsible for checking that line managers are adhering to specified personnel policies and procedures.

Case law: the body of precedent which builds up as statutes and company policies are interpreted in particular cases. (May also be referred to as *custom and practice*.)

Certificate in Personnel Practice: one year part-time introduction to the skills of personnel management, offered by colleges and training providers on behalf of the Institute of Personnel Management.

Coaching: a process of 'learning by doing' whereby the boss delegates tasks or projects and acts as a 'sounding board' for the trainee – who works out how best to tackle the task and sees it through.

Co-equal professional (role): one in which the personnel manager is accepted as a member of the organization's management team – on equal terms with line managers and other professionals.

Collective bargaining: process whereby management and trade union representatives negotiate terms and conditions and procedures governing employment.

Competence: the skills and knowledge, gained through education, training and experience, required to perform a job satisfactorily.

Contract of employment: the terms and conditions by which employer and employee agree to abide. A written statement of these must be issued within thirteen weeks of the beginning of employment.

Corporate planning: the systematic process of developing long-term strategies and plans to achieve defined business objectives.

Cost of living increase: an adjustment to salary based directly or indirectly on the rate of inflation. (May also be referred to as *annual reviews*.)

Counselling: a process whereby employees are encouraged to discuss personal and/or work-related problems with someone (their boss, a personnel specialist or a welfare counsellor), with a view to finding their own best solution.

Curriculum Vitae: a statement of education, work experience and training acquired to date and of personal attributes likely to be relevant to prospective employers.

Development: the process whereby the competences of employees are developed to enable them to take on bigger or wider roles in future.

Disciplinary procedure: set of guidelines for helping to put right problems with an employee's performance or conduct.

Discrimination: decisions based on particular characteristics. This is unlawful if those characteristics include race, sex or marital status.

Dispute: a complaint against the employer, raised collectively by a group of employees or their trade union representatives.

Employee benefits: deferred payments, such as pensions, and non-cash payments, such as holidays, company car, uniform, which form part of the contract of employment.

Employee relations: the relationship between employers and their employees. The formal aspects of this relationship may be conducted through representatives from employers' organizations or federations and trade unions. This is often referred to as *industrial relations.*

Employee services: additional activities or services provided voluntarily by employers to improve the quality of employees' lives (rather than as part of the contract of employment). Examples include stress counselling and recreational facilities.

Evaluation (of training): assessment of the extent to which the specific objectives of a training programme have been met. May be carried out at a number of levels – from individual enjoyment to impact on profitability.

Executive (role): one in which the personnel manager is authorized to make decisions which are binding on line management.

Grading structure: hierarchy of payment bands – usually related to the relative importance of the jobs concerned.

Grievance: a complaint against the employer, raised personally by an employee.

Harmonization: process of bringing all employee groups within the scope of one pay structure and one set of terms and conditions of employment.

Human resource management: the strategic approach to the acquisition, motivation, development and management of the organization's human resources.

Human resource planning: the process of planning the numbers and skills required to enable the organization to achieve its objectives.

Incentive schemes: methods of motivating employees to improve performance through the promise of additional financial rewards or prizes.

Industrial action: strikes, picketing, working to rule, sit-ins and other forms of sanction used by employees to persuade employers to concede to their collective demands.

Industrial relations: see employee relations.

Industrial tribunal: a three-person panel, comprised of a legally qualified chairperson and employer and trade union representatives, which hears individual claims of breaches in employers' legal obligations to their employees. Tribunals can impose financial penalties on employers and/or order them to take back employees who have been unfairly dismissed.

Institute of Personnel Management: the professional body for personnel practitioners. It provides information, professional education and updating and advice to members. Full membership is gained via the professional education scheme.

Job description: a statement of the main purpose, key results to be achieved, and main tasks to be carried out by the holder of a particular job, and a description of the context and conditions under which it is to be performed.

Job design: the process of determining the content of a particular job.

Job evaluation: the process of determining the relative worth of different jobs – by reference to the content of the jobs themselves.

Labour market: the supply of and demand for particular categories of employee, within particular geographic areas.

Labour turnover: the number of employees who leave the employment of a particular employer in the course of a year – usually expressed as a percentage of the average number in employment during the course of the year.

Learning objectives: a statement of what a trainee should be able to do, that is what competences he or she will be able to demonstrate, at the end of a training programme, course or piece of instruction. It should be observable and, if possible measurable, and should define the standard of performance required.

Line managers: managers who are responsible for a mainstream activity which directly impacts on the results achieved by the organization.

Motivation: an attempt to understand the needs and drives which prompt people to act in particular ways and to provide ways of helping them to satisfy these within the context of work.

National Vocational Qualification (NVQ): a certificate of competence in a particular field of work, which conforms to a nationally determined standard.

Negotiation: process of discussion between management and union representatives leading to agreement over procedural or substantive issues.

Organization design: process of determining the overall structure of, and reporting, relationships within an organization.

Pay survey: study of rates of pay and benefits offered by other employers for particular categories of employee.

Payment structure: pattern of internal differentials between the pay levels for various jobs (often expressed as a series of grades).

Payroll department: department responsible for calculating and paying wages or salaries and administering National Insurance and Pay As You Earn income tax (PAYE).

Performance appraisal: regular review of the way in which an individual is performing his or her job. It usually takes the form of an interview between boss (appraiser) and subordinate (appraisee) and is recorded in a written report.

Performance related pay (PRP): payment system where part or all of the employee's pay is linked directly to the achievement of specified performance standards.

Personnel information system: method used for compiling and storing the collection of employee records used as the basis for statistical calculation and monitoring. Computerized personnel information systems are usually referred to as CPIS.

Personnel requisition: document used to request authority to recruit a new employee.

Personnel service: the provision of help and support to line managers by undertaking routine work, such as the writing of recruitment advertisements, which would be time-consuming for line managers to do for themselves.

Personnel specification: statement of the competences and other attributes deemed necessary for the successful performance of a particular job.

Policy: framework for decision-making, usually laid down by the board of directors.

Premium payments: additional payments made to employees to compensate for service above and beyond that which is generally required – such as shift working or overtime.

Proactive: taking the initiative in introducing change, rather than waiting until change is inevitable.

Procedural agreement: agreement between employer and trade union regarding the way in which particular issues, such as disciplinary matters and grievances, are to be dealt with.

Professional Education Scheme (PES): programme of full- or part-time study leading to graduate membership of the Institute of Personnel Management and thence to full membership.

Psychometric tests: assessment devices used to measure particular traits, abilities and aptitudes.

Recruitment: process of attracting a field of candidates.

Redundancy: dismissal on the grounds that the employer's requirement for particular categories of employee has diminished.

Rewards: pay, benefits and other forms of remuneration paid to an employee in return for his or her work.

Selection: process of choosing which candidate best meets the personnel specification for a particular post.

Selection criteria: the factors, such as specific competences or attributes, which underlie selection decisions.

Shop steward: trade union representative in the workplace.

Substantive agreement: agreement between employer and trade union representatives regarding specific terms and conditions of employment, such as pay, pensions, holidays.

Technology based training (TBT): the use of computer programs (CBT), interactive video (IV), compact disc interactive (CD-1) and other technologically-based training methods.

Terms and conditions of employment: the basis upon which employer and employee enter into a contract of employment. They include pay, hours of work, sick pay entitlement, pension arrangements and the other rights and obligations of the parties to the contract.

Trade union: organization set up to represent people working in a particular trade or industry in their dealings with their employers.

Training: process of helping people to acquire the competences needed for successful performance of their present jobs. It may take place during the course of normal working (on-job training) or away from the workplace (off-job training).

Training and Enterprise Council (TEC): government-funded groups of employers whose general brief is to encourage the development of the training and other initiatives necessary to ensure the availability of the competences which will be required by local industry in future.

Training gap: the difference between the skills and knowledge which an employee possesses, and those needed for successful performance of the job.

Training needs analysis: process of working out what training is needed by particular individuals or groups of employees.

Training programme: a series of activities, either on or off-job (or both), designed to help an individual achieve a specified set of learning objectives.

Index